CONFESSIONS OF A
CRYPTO
MILLIONAIRE

CONFESSIONS OF A
CRYPTO
MILLIONAIRE

*My Unlikely Escape
from Corporate America*

DAN CONWAY

ZEALOT

Published by Zealot Publishing
1325 Howard Avenue #920
Burlingame, CA 94010

ISBN: 978-1-7331717-0-0 (print)
978-1-7331717-1-7 (audio book)
978-1-7331717-2-4 (ebook)

DEDICATION

To my sister Maureen O'Rourke, who
called bullshit and laid it all on the line.

CONTENTS

AUTHOR'S NOTE

Due to non-disclosure agreements, I have fictionalized the content in this book relating to Acme Corporation. I describe my experience working at a big company, but it is not a description of any particular company. I've changed company structure and events, details about the people and consultants who work there, and significant additional information relating to Acme. As a result, this content does not portray my actual experience. Every person in the book relating to Acme is effectively a composite character, not a description of any particular person. I've done this on the advice of legal counsel. My intent is not to make up events, add fake drama, or create a false narrative. It is simply to describe my time at Acme Corporation so that it is not a description of any one company where I was employed during my career.

Everything else in this book happened as described, including all of the personal events during my time at Acme, and everything before and after. I've done my best to faithfully relate my memory of events. As with all memories, I can only attest that this is how I remember and interpret everything I've written about.

While all individuals described relating to Acme are fake, I've also changed the names of real people throughout the book to protect their privacy: my former co-worker at Blanc & Otus, "Cindy"; "George" and "Gene" at Wells Fargo; my family friend "Carlo"; the financial advisor "Carl"; the Italian restaurant owners, "Ennio" and "Martina"; the Italian driver "Matteo"; our friends "Rebecca," "Stan," and "Larry"; r/EthTraders "Steven," "Tracy," "Ryan," "John," and "Pelayo." In addition, these are made-up surnames to describe real families: Taylor, Foster, Sullivan, Pattner, Vice, Shiner. In a few instances, I've changed identifying details for these people and families to further screen their identities.

Although I write in detail about my experiences in cryptocurrency and other financial and business matters, this is a memoir and a commentary rather than a book of business advice. Readers who are seeking information and advice about business matters should consult resources other than this book.

As a style point, throughout this book I capitalize Bitcoin and Ethereum when I refer to their blockchains. I do not capitalize bitcoin and ether when I refer to these currencies.

PROLOGUE

When the *Financial Times* interviewed me for a story about cryptocurrency millionaires in March 2018, I told them the unvarnished truth:

"I invested because I wanted the underdogs to win, for once—losers like me who didn't make the rules and didn't have the money… We'd been forced to tweet corporate philanthropy hashtags, and we weren't going to take it anymore."

Even while I was working my way up the ladder, I felt like an alien in corporate America. The bureaucracy, chains of command and emphasis on fake company culture made me and most of my co-workers miserable. It brought out the worst in us. It also appeared to be a crappy way to get things done.

This is not a groundbreaking insight. Eighty-five percent of people hate their jobs, according to a 2017 Gallup study. Movies like *Office Space*, *The Matrix,* and *9 to 5* became cult hits by pointing out the obvious. Modern work sucks.

Sadly, I was never a superachiever capable of grabbing early retirement-level money. Nor was I able to follow a path leading me away from corporate America. Throughout my career, escape was always on my mind, though I had limited means to achieve it.

Then I discovered Bitcoin and Ethereum, technologies based on an entirely new organizing principle. A priesthood of true believers said cryptocurrencies could disrupt the banks, corporations, and other organizations that ran society. Or at least provide an alternative to them. I could fund these networks by buying bitcoin and ether, the cryptocurrencies that power their blockchains. I could help change the world and get rich ... not necessarily in that order.

The Onion has created a helpful guide to this new technology. It begins with a simple Q&A:

Q: What is Blockchain?

A: Do you want to talk science shit or do you want to make some fucking money?

First, the science shit (and some history).

The double-entry ledger was invented in 1340. It was a way for merchants to easily track their credits and debt. This enabled them to centrally plan their businesses for the first time. Economists believe the double-entry ledger spawned modern capitalism and, thus, the modern corporation.

In 2009, Bitcoin introduced the world to blockchain, the first triple-entry ledger. It allows an infinite number of participants to do business on a public ledger that is self-settling. Since this ledger isn't controlled by any one party, it is decentralized. Financial transactions and, theoretically, any type of complex business can be completed on the Bitcoin, Ethereum or other public blockchain ledgers.

The big-picture implications of the triple-entry ledger are huge. Today, the world economy is controlled by corporations and banks running centrally controlled double-entry ledgers. The Internet was supposed to be free, but even it has been captured. The FAANG companies (Facebook,

Apple, Amazon, Netflix, and Google) have made it a gated community.

Blockchain is an opportunity to organize in a different way. It has the potential to weaken the gatekeepers, rule makers, and monopolies through decentralization. In the years and decades ahead, it gives us a shot to revolutionize institutions the way double-entry bookkeeping did seven hundred years ago.

And it might let outsiders like me storm the castle.

Now, to the fucking money.

My story involves large sums of money. When the boom was on, I felt like Pablo Escobar, with a chirpy attitude and a closet full of dad jeans. But my story is messy and unconventional.

I'm not a traditional tech bro who struck it rich by getting in early. I had a lot more to lose when I went down the rabbit hole. I was a forty-four-year-old father of three with a conventional life on the edge of the Silicon Valley bubble. My marriage was still recovering from my past battles with demons.

I've always had a hard time distinguishing between living life to the fullest, and selfish, self- destructive behavior like drinking too much, risking too much, and obsessing too much on any one thing as a way to make me feel different.

The particular culture of my family also played a role. My sister Kathleen, pumped her 401(k) into penny stocks during the dot-com boom. On a dare, my brother jumped off a bridge so high up that when they fished him out of the water with two broken ribs and a concussion, he was investigated for attempted suicide. And my grandfather left everything he knew in Ireland and started over in America, without a penny to his name.

It turns out that my entire identity, everything about my character and family, both admirable and loathsome—every intelligent insight, selfish and self-destructive impulse, every twist of professional fate—had prepared me for crypto.

CHAPTER ONE

CLIMBING THE LADDER

August 10, 2010

I swiveled my chair one hundred eighty degrees between the two sides of my desk, which surrounded me. I'd practiced this move absentmindedly for five years in this same Safeway headquarters work space. Each time I landed in front of my computer, I hit refresh. I was jonesing to hear the ping of the incoming email that would change my life.

I was hoping to get an offer for a big job at Acme Corporation, a golden ticket.

My head throbbed a little bit, but I was used to that. Two years prior, in 2008, I had started drinking again after a ten-year hiatus, imposed after I blacked out at a San Francisco nightclub in my mid-twenties. I'd punched a security guard who was trying to eject me from the club and received a well-deserved Rodney King-style beating from the other bouncers. I was arrested for misdemeanor assault. The charges were eventually dropped, but I was sufficiently scared and ashamed to quit drinking for good. Or at least for ten years.

During those sober years, I'd married Eileen. Together, we'd bought a nice three-bedroom, one-bath house in Burlingame on the northern edge of Silicon Valley. By 2007, we'd added two kids to the operation: two-year-old Danny and infant Annie. Eileen told me that by 2009, we'd have three kids.

Suddenly, the urge to blow off steam was overwhelming. I was worn out by the one-two punch of parenting and trying to get ahead in my career. After my hour-long commute home through stop-and-go traffic, I was exhausted. I really wanted to enjoy jumping on the floor with my kids and pretending to be a goat. It broke my heart that it was the most difficult part of my day.

Malicious logic from the dark side suggested that I should loosen up with a few drinks. Maybe stop declining invitations to the six-bottles-of-wine dinner parties that were a staple of the hot elementary school-parent social scene we'd just been introduced to. Maybe I'd be more carefree, less priestly. It had been ten years, for God's sake. I had grown up. Eileen had never seen me drink and was against the idea, but she didn't leave me when I started drinking. More on that later.

Refresh, refresh, refresh.

I was far enough into my career to know the golden ticket email might not come through. But I thought it would. I was outstanding in interviews. I knew how to showcase my intelligent, personable, and ready-for-public-office side. The side that got inspired, did its homework, and didn't settle, which, in my line of work, meant landing high-value media placements for the products or initiatives at the companies where I worked. That was the holy grail of success in public relations, my career niche.

At my first job at public relations firm Blanc & Otus in the mid-1990s, I was the best media pitcher. Through tenacity, I once landed three stories in the *San Francisco Chronicle* over a weekend and was rewarded with a round of applause on Monday morning. That moment is enshrined in the *Dan Conway: Reliving the Moment History* exhibit, open 24/7 in my mind. A few years later, at PeopleSoft, I won the Outstanding Contributor Award, which entitled the winner to five hundred stock options and an awkward hug on stage with shy billionaire CEO Dave Duffield.

In interviews, I showcased this side of my character and tried my best to hide Flip Side, the bed-wetting, escapist gimp with bad judgment who lives in the basement of my personality. Flip Side knew to shut the fuck up during interviews. He could roam around later.

Flip Side was born when I was in seventh grade and struggling through what I now realize was an acute adolescent depression. I suddenly no longer knew what to say to anyone. Life was replaced with silence, like I was a deaf person watching a movie without hearing aids or closed captions. I thought all of my hair was going to fall out (it did, decades later). My friends abandoned me and thoughtfully organized a "Hate Dan Day." Then I recovered in high school, where I was elected class president twice, was prom king, and wrote my own column in the high school newspaper, "Conway's Corner."

But Flip Side returned and took up permanent residence during my next profound depression, which struck like liquid death my freshman year of college. While loud music and the sounds of towels snapping and other college hijinks seeped under my dorm room door, I lay on my bed and stared out the window at the living creatures walking by.

I also drank. A lot. After waking up on the bathroom floor of a fraternity house in a river of piss one too many times, I realized I might have a problem.

I emerged on the other side of my depressions through grit and, eventually, medication, but sober or not, I now had Flip Side as a companion. He was a devil that told me I was a real loser and that I needed something outside of myself to make me happy. In addition to substances, he hungered for diversions, dreams and recognition, even though he got nervous and screwed me up when I might have achieved those things.

Refresh, refresh, refresh.

There was an email. Crap, it was a note from my boss asking if I could meet at 3:00 p.m. I responded that I could. He wanted to discuss our fourth-quarter communications wrap-up report, a difficult, grueling project that resulted in a thirty-page document no one read. It allowed us to make the case up the chain that we needed as much or more funding for our department the following year. I'd have to work for several weeks writing the damn thing, which wouldn't win me any praise or promotion, just a go-ahead to do everything we'd been doing again next year.

Refresh, refresh, refresh.

Down the hall, I heard the *clop, clop, clop* of contact on formica. I looked around the corner. An intern from the breakfast food division was dropping boxes of trail mix bars on each desk. At Safeway, this windfall happened just about every week. A can of peas, a stove cleaner, or another new or discontinued product would show up on all of our desks when we arrived for work. Eileen was always thrilled when I came home with these random items, not for monetary reasons, but because they brought back memories of her childhood. Having grown up in North Andover, Massachusetts, in a big middle-class Irish-Italian-American family, she was nostalgic about stories of things "falling off a truck": a case of peaches, a box of purses, forty pounds of frozen beef. She would mention my canned-good treasures at dinner parties with our rich or becoming-rich tech industry friends while I stared on in shame.

Our friends had started to pull away from us financially. Some worked at Apple, Facebook, and Google. Their stock options alone were worth more than my salary at Safeway. Eileen and I stopped being able to participate in conversations about their latest vacations and luxury cars. We agreed that they were becoming shallow by discussing things we couldn't afford.

Refresh, refresh, refresh.

Do they track these things, the number of times you hit refresh? I wondered.

Another email came through, a meeting appointment. *Let's get together to review public messaging for the packaging initiative.*

A meeting I hoped I'd never have to attend.

It wasn't that I was miserable at Safeway. The company had been good to me. But I'd hit a ceiling and needed to move on to get any higher. We needed the money, and I wanted the recognition.

There were moments when I thought I'd hit it big there, get to an executive level, and earn the bucks and attention I craved. The high point came when I devised a plastic bag strategy that would be good for the environment, save the company millions of dollars and spare us pressure from left-leaning interest groups. I traveled to Ireland with a group of Safeway experts to study their progressive plastic bag laws. I dined in the Irish Senate. I studied everything and came home with a fully formed plan that I thought could change our company, the entire grocery industry, and my future.

A week later, my palms were sweaty, and I was presenting around a gorgeous boardroom table to Safeway CEO Steve Burd and five other top executives. My boss's boss, a woman who didn't suffer fools, was also there. She looked nervous. She'd seen the full measure of me. I'd spent hours with her in my car, shepherding her to various executive events. She'd seen me speak with confidence, crack the perfect joke. She'd also seen me fumble a storyline, flash self-doubt when expressing an opinion. In short, she'd seen my Flip Side jumping in to foul up my image in a cloud of insecurity.

But now, in this room, I was full of energy, and I laid out a perfectly simple plan, a win-win that I'd studied and knew inside and out. I could see that I had the attention of the execs by the way they responded to the slight humor I'd added to my deck. I lost myself in the content, in the gist of what I was saying, and that momentum prevented any doubt from creeping in.

When I finished, Steve said, "Great Job, Dan. This is going to help us find a path forward." My boss's boss held my eyes for a moment as I said thank you and exited the room, letting them move on to other executive matters. She looked pleased and a little surprised.

A few weeks later, I was invited to join Steve and a few other big shots as they traveled to our Denver division to discuss plastic bags. This was a big deal, an undeniable sign that they were grooming me for something bigger. We walked into the cavernous room where several hundred employees were already assembled and waiting for our arrival. The room broke into applause, an ode to Steve. Damn, that felt good.

On the return flight, still high from the sudden muscular liftoff of the small jet as we soared over the Rockies, I got too chatty with Steve, asking about his family and telling him about mine. Later, my manager told me I'd violated Steve's personal space. I was mortified. The spell was broken. Safeway eventually adopted my plastic bag policy, but I never regained the confidence that showed I was ready for the big leagues. I knew another opportunity might not come along.

Refresh, refresh, refresh.

But that was a thing of the past. I'd have a fresh start. Because there was the email. Acme was going to make me an offer. I'd gotten the job.

CHAPTER TWO

DELIVERANCE

I heard about the Acme position from an acquaintance and had been quietly interviewing for months. He said the pay would be $250,000 salary plus bonus, restricted stock options and other benefits. I was making $130,000 at Safeway, so this was an enormous step up the economic ladder. It was also the perfect time for us to receive a windfall.

Our finances had been blowtorched by the 2008 financial crisis, and we were still struggling to recover. After Annie was born in March 2007, Eileen left her full-time gig heading up a PR agency and started a one-person consulting practice. She worked from our kitchen table in between duties at our preschool co-op. When the carnage and bank failures started in 2008, she lost half her clients overnight. One of her clients, a man in his mid-fifties, sent her a note: *I'm sorry, but everything is on hold, and I'm not sure I am even going to keep my job.* He didn't.

She fought like hell to stabilize a much-smaller business amid scary news coverage and economic paranoia. Companies were hoarding money and preparing for a global depression. In that environment, which lasted for years, it was impossible to grow the business back to what we needed to be financially stable.

Eileen and I didn't have any liquid savings. We were scraping to pay our $5,000 mortgage each month in addition to our regular bills at Target, Pizza My Heart, Pacific Gas & Electric and the like. Our cushion was the equity line of credit on our house, which we used to supplement our monthly income as needed. It was also our emergency fund if I lost my job or we were hit with some other financial catastrophe.

Then our mortgage holder, Wells Fargo, pulled our equity line of credit. They claimed our house was worth 30 percent less than it had been the day before. The housing market was in decline, thanks in no small measure to Wells Fargo's enthusiastic participation in the subprime mortgage bubble. They justified rescinding the equity line of credit on our prime-status mortgage, and those of thousands of other homebuyers, by sending drive-by estimators all over Northern California. They zoomed by and took a few pictures, but they never knocked on any doors. The shoddy "estimates" of lower-appraised values were full of errors and template descriptions written in their corporate office.

We were able to survive by tightening our belts, holding to a budget and using credit card debt as needed. Other than visits to Eileen's parents on the East Coast, we weren't taking vacations. I continued driving a variety of piece-of-shit cars while Eileen drove our "good" car, a Honda Odyssey minivan.

We were still better off financially than most people in the country, and we weren't exactly falling head-first into poverty. We were still officially upper class. But it didn't feel that way each time we had to buy a new furnace, fix a banged-up fender or handle the other unpredictable expenses that seemed to come more frequently as our family grew.

★ ★ ★

The promise of this Acme salary stirred a theme that had been building since I entered the workforce fifteen years before. I'd get out if I could. If I somehow accumulated enough "fuck-you money"—an amount high enough to say "fuck you" to your boss on the way out the door, if you so desired—I'd take it.

I'd tried my hand at escape once before, in 1998. I left a job at PeopleSoft totally burned out at twenty-seven, resigning a few months after winning the Outstanding Contributor Award. I'd spent the previous year in my cubicle, working my ass off. I had no personal life. There was too much work to pay attention to anything else.

It was an existential crisis, at a time when I could still afford to have one.

I read the book *Your Money or Your Life* and was inspired by it. Co-author Joe Dominguez explained the idea, which was to establish financial independence over time by burning both ends of the candle, reducing all spending drastically, as if your life depended on it (it does, he implores) and making as much money as you could, saving nearly all of it. I decided to save all of my treasure and build up enough money to win early financial independence. I'd live a simple but free life.

Another book inspired me back then: *Into the Wild* by Jon Krakauer. It details the story of Chris McCandless, a young man who rejects society, gives up his possessions and hitchhikes across the country to the wild Alaskan outback to make it on his own. McCandless couldn't accept modern life. I couldn't accept modern work. I decided to give up my apartment, sell my car and move back home with my parents.

Those who encountered McCandless on his journey remembered his small wisdoms and transcendent spirit. He donated all of the money in his bank account to OXFAM and burned the remaining cash in his wallet. During my vision quest, I berated a bank teller over a small fee and asked my father if he could please stop *accidentally* opening my mail, because it seemed to be happening a lot. I was twenty-eight years old.

My plan was to drastically reduce my spending and start a one-person PR consulting practice that would generate $10,000 per month or more. I'd sock it away, bite the bullet and accumulate enough so I had options for how I'd live the rest of my life.

I figured I'd eventually get a small, rent-controlled apartment in the Mission District of San Francisco and keep it for decades or move to Eureka up north, a low-cost-of-living destination full of Bay Area cast-offs I'd visited a few times. I could write for a living, start a small one-person business, or find some other way to make enough money to live frugally without having to rejoin the traditional workforce.

I consumed extreme frugality newsletters for inspiration and lifestyle ideas. The *Tightwad Gazette* was particularly good reading. The author was dead-set against any spending at all. She explained how one could cut out common, chronic expenses like gas bills by riding a bike to work. I followed many of her suggestions and absorbed one hundred percent of the spirit in which they were made. This was enough to make me what you might call "cheap."

I remember shopping for a good friend's wedding present at a brightly lit Pottery Barn in the mall, a rare shopping expedition. I blinked at the price. I could live for a month for the cost of the potpourri. The only thing left on the registry was a set of eight wine glasses, for a total cost of $95, which was more than the $80 I was willing to spend. So I only purchased seven glasses. When the bride opened my gift at the after-wedding party for close friends, she thought that Pottery Barn had screwed up until she figured out I'd only given up to my budgeted amount.

Each budget-saving task, like making your own glue with cornstarch and vinegar, was straightforward. But a lifestyle based on extreme budgeting was isolating, unless you counted the company of Mom and Dad in the next room, wondering if you might be ready to announce your mental health diagnosis.

Some people in my position might have pursued a career as a contractor, electrician, or other high-paying blue-collar job. My money-making skills outside of office work were limited.

From a young age, I knew I'd better become a college boy, or else. Growing up, my family had a cabin in Russian River in Sonoma County, which everyone referred to as the River. It served as a training ground for me, my brother, and cousins as we learned to fix things with our hands and become capable men. At least they did. I couldn't build a deck, fix a door, or assemble a barbecue. While the rest of them mastered the tactics of being handy and moved on to the blue-collar brain work of envisioning a new kitchen and then making it so, I was relegated to digging holes, carrying heavy things, and making a lovely lunch. I'd come home from Georgetown, where I was earning honors grades, and resume my duties as family dunce at the cabin, spreading manure for our new garden and carrying bags of cement up three flights of stairs.

During this stint of living at home, my one-person consulting practice was going well. I was making good money and socking it all away with very few expenses. Then my resolve slipped away imperceptibly. I talked to a friend who was working for an Internet company and doing just great. He'd recently gotten back from a business trip to Japan and Australia. His stock options might make him rich in a few years. He'd just had a threesome!

Ever so slightly, without thought or intention, I started to drift. My mooring had dissolved—it had been secured with sand, not cement.

Then Macromedia came calling. They wanted to hire me to be the PR Manager for Flash, their popular web graphics product. I could take the job and get my own apartment again. I'd rejoin the people I'd been traveling with my whole life. The familiar crowd. Meet some chicks. Maybe I could make it in the corporate world, after all.

So I accepted.

A few months after I started at Macromedia, I was told I'd be getting a new boss. A hotshot who'd previously headed up the Apple account at Edelman PR. She'd apparently gone to Brown. Her name was Eileen Stanley. She was my age. My ego preferred my bosses to be at least ten to fifteen years older than me.

We started working together, and it was good. She was the most productive person I'd ever encountered. She could write a whole report in a few hours and put together an international product launch plan in an evening. She was lightning smart, good with people, and not at all snotty. She was humble and nice. And attractive, with short blond hair, high cheekbones and nice legs. And she liked my jokes.

Over the wall of my cubicle, I heard Eileen talking to her mom on the phone. It sounded just like me talking to my parents.

"Ok, Mom, well, I thought you said you knew when I was landing. You don't have to come pick me up at all if you don't want to."

They were bickering.

"Ok, I can't wait to see you guys, either. But tell Dad I refuse to watch the History Channel this time."

Then "I love you," before saying goodbye.

Our group took a team-building trip to Disneyland. Eileen sang the "Small World" theme song in a little girl's voice during the ride. At first I thought she was being ironic, but no—she didn't even notice me staring. She was just enthralled with the wonder of Small World. Hilarious. Also … adorable.

All six of us on the team headed for the Matterhorn. Back then, before Disneyland went through a sexual-harassment upgrade, riders on the Matterhorn had to straddle each other. It was like two people on a horse, except the back person's legs wrapped all the way in front of the lead rider. It was a position you might find in a tantric sex book. Eileen and I shared a car. It was good for me. I began to desire an encounter outside of team meetings.

We'd be going back and forth on press release edits, but I kept thinking of another type of back and forth. If only we were two primates in the jungle rather than people pretending to be civilized professionals, the deed would have already been done. (I've always been a romantic.)

Then we went on a business trip to New York, which turned out to be close enough. We rented a car and drove to the Hamptons. We stayed at a bed-and-breakfast owned by a guy named Prince or Earl or Duke, we can never remember which, and had a hell of a good time. Soon after, I left Macromedia, erasing our dating-at-work problem.

In subsequent years, and especially after Danny was born, I temporarily abandoned the idea of retiring early by extreme budgeting or any other alternative lifestyle. Having kids changed everything. No matter how jaded or frustrated I might've been, the sight of my kids sleeping in their beds had a chilling effect on my existential misgivings. I really wanted them to be happy and have an excellent start to life.

Now, as I awaited my offer from Acme with Eileen by my side, twelve years after my first attempt to exit corporate America, we'd be pursuing financial independence together, although Eileen didn't like to talk about money. If I could keep getting raises and stock options, we could pile up cash to do something outside of the corporate grind in the years ahead.

During this period, I'd been able to control my drinking. Although I was often the drunkest person at any party, the home and work pressures were proving to be enough to keep me in line. Now that we wouldn't have to worry about money, things were looking up. In addition to saving for early retirement, perhaps we'd take a few luxurious trips and buy "timepieces." We'd definitely be enjoying more locally sourced organic vegetables, grass-fed beef, and freshly ground, individually pressed coffee.

We'd be like the parents of my rich-kid friends growing up, the ones with cushy jobs in corporate America rather than in public education, like my dad, or part-time retail, like my mom. These parents bought their kids golf and tennis lessons and dropped them off at Outward Bound camp in their BMWs. I was lucky to go to Benihana at birthday time.

It wasn't just the money. With this Acme job, I hoped to graduate and escape the overcrowded herd of mid-level staffers that populate LinkedIn. Many smart and deserving people never climb any higher up the pyramid. They toil away in the middle ranks their whole careers, losing hair and adding waist while holding onto that part of their youth that allows them to gaze admiringly into the eyes of a manager ten years their junior. They never get the chance to go to Italy on vacation, develop their own "management style," or shop at the fancy boutique t-shirt store on Burlingame Avenue. They never get to be cool.

At past jobs, I'd always been the one briefing more senior people, writing their messaging, and wracking my brain to come up with insights for their consideration before important meetings. Now I'd be the one getting briefed. I no longer had to worry about the knock on the door. I'd be the one knocking.

I felt dignified and gangster. Also scared shitless.

Acme is one of the largest companies in America. When I joined in 2010, there were more than two hundred thousand employees in more than a dozen countries. This corporate behemoth was comprised of colossal business units across global geographies and operated more than two thousand retail stores in the United States. I'd be an executive, with a full team and a substantial salary.

I'd hit the big time.

***

I was told my offer letter was working its way through the system and would come any day. I drifted through my days at Safeway like a cadaver, every ounce of motivation and work ethic drained since the moment I knew I was leaving.

The letter came, offering a $150,000 salary, modest options, and a bonus if all targets were met. The salary represented a 15 percent raise over Safeway. But they'd promised $250,000, a 92 percent raise!

Except they hadn't promised me anything. The guy who turned me onto the job had no actual knowledge of the salary. He guessed wrong, trying to make things sound as good as possible.

To the vast majority of people in this country, a salary of $150,000 is tremendous. But in the Bay Area, with a mortgage on a million-dollar house, three kids, and the expenses of an upper middle-class life (gym, summer camps, vacations), that salary wouldn't erase our money worries. We'd still be trying to figure out how to pay for three college educations and fund our retirement. It was more money than I was making, but it wouldn't change our lives like a glorious $120,000 salary bump.

Sometimes people only get one big break in their careers, when the stars align and a sweet job with long-term financial security falls into their laps. This was my shot. The jackpot had revealed itself, and I could climb the corporate ranks after years of toil. I was prepared to buckle down and work my ass off, sell my soul, sacrifice every passion until retirement, which would hopefully come sooner rather than later.

But I wanted to be compensated accordingly. Even before I started, I knew this post would come with grand headaches, difficulties, and frustrations. As a vice president at

Acme, I'd be in charge of the communications and political strategy for the company's biggest market. I'd have a multi-million-dollar budget and manage five employees, a handful of contractors, and three public relations agencies. I'd be the lead political counselor to the top Acme executives in the state. It was a big-time job, with big-time pressures and the distinct possibility of failure. I was furious that I wasn't being offered a big-time salary. I tried to negotiate. They wouldn't budge a dollar.

The delicate dance between company and prospective hire, which is supposed to culminate in big smiles, a signed job acceptance letter, and introductions all around, was breaking down.

My future bosses were surprised by my pushback and clearly didn't appreciate it. They said, "This always happens with Californians!"

Yes, I thought. *I apologize for living where a three-bedroom home costs more than four goats and a half-cup of Grandma Opie's teeth.* Living in the Bay Area was expensive, and I expected Acme to factor that into their calculations. From their perspective, I was shouting and pounding my high chair because I hadn't received enough Grey Poupon—and it smelled like I had a dirty diaper.

My hiring manager bit her tongue and had me call an HR representative to continue the dialogue.

This was my first experience with a concept called Acme Unified. Acme is a massive spaceship, with rows of cubicles on various decks devoted to handling specific functions. In this case, my compensation specialist was charged with explaining the salary package. Unfortunately, Employee 1342 in his Denver cubicle didn't know much about the job offer, and he couldn't explain how the restricted stock program worked. He was cranky as hell.

None of it worked, because Acme is a mish-mash of regional companies that have been pieced together through acquisitions over decades. Each company's processes had been smashed into the centralized structure that has governed Acme forever. This is the same structure Acme helped pioneer and that virtually every corporation utilizes to this day, including Google, Facebook, and other tech darlings that pretend to be more decentralized.

The point of Unified Acme was to make all of the company's 245,000 employees less surly and idiotic to each other. The goal was to pull the masses of a massive company together, systems-wise and culture-wise, to avoid situations like this.

Ultimately, what was I going to do? Decline the job, stay at Safeway for $20,000 less per year, and forego the big title and bigger stage that Acme offered? At least I'd be working closer to home, in downtown San Francisco rather than the East Bay. This was probably the same calculus the company used when formulating the offer in the first place. I told myself to buck up, and I did. It was still a step in the right direction, and I'd work my way to a higher salary eventually. I accepted the job.

CHAPTER THREE

CYPHERPUNKS

While my focus in the years after the financial crisis was to climb as high as I could in the establishment, a group of zealots called the cypherpunks were challenging the establishment.

These computer scientists, political-edge cases, and contrarians were concerned about privacy and personal liberty. They believed that corporations and governments had become too powerful. They'd been communicating with one another for years through an email list that had been going strong since the first days of the Internet Bulletin Board System in the 1980s.

The cypherpunks considered cryptography to be an important tool for thwarting surveillance. They developed new ways for people to communicate using digital cyphers, which required the use of private keys.

In the mid-2000s, computer networks became exponentially more powerful, and social media introduced the world to new data-mining vulnerabilities. By that time, many of the cypherpunks had created organizations that were fighting for libertarian policies in the courts and on the Internet.

In Washington D.C., cypherpunk Mitch Kapor's Electronic Frontier Foundation was battling AOL at the

Federal Trade Commission, alleging AOL engaged in deceptive and unfair trade practices by disclosing the search queries of 650,000 users.

In Silicon Valley, cypherpunk Bram Cohen's peer-to-peer file sharing program, BitTorrent, had drawn blood from big telecom in 2006, after Comcast had throttled the BitTorrent service. Cohen, who self-diagnosed his Asperger's Syndrome, sued and won a federal lawsuit, one of the first skirmishes in the net neutrality war.

The cypherpunks were outstanding at coming up with new ways to send *information* privately, but they struggled to find a way to transact *value* privately. A functional underground community required that two parties be able to conduct business outside of surveillance. If their messages were private but their exchange of digital money was not, the entire transaction was still compromised.

They believed the answer would be found by utilizing distributed computing, which uses multiple unconnected computers to complete a task. They worked on different ways to establish a public ledger (i.e., a third-party ledger) that was maintained by multiple nodes (computers) and did not rely on any one party to validate the exchange. In a distributed—or decentralized—system, if any node was compromised, the remaining untainted nodes could still ensure the transaction was completed.

It was an elusive goal, and they had several false starts. The Hashcash and Digicash projects achieved breakthroughs but ultimately didn't work. The two most difficult challenges were removing every single point of failure and preventing "double spends," which could occur if the same money was sent to two different parties.

In October 2008, a person or persons named Satoshi Nakamoto sent an email to the cypherpunk email list, introducing Bitcoin. He said he'd solved the digital money problem. He attached a nine-page white paper explaining how he'd done it.

"In this paper, we propose a solution to the double-spending problem using a peer-to-peer distributed timestamp server to generate computational proof of the chronological order of transactions."

Satoshi proposed that each peer-to-peer transaction be arranged into a block of transactions. It would then be chained to the previous block by the node that wins a race to solve a computational puzzle. The winning node receives bitcoin in return. In this way, bitcoin was an entirely new currency that would be distributed to the computers that added their power to the network. As Satoshi wrote, *"The steady addition of a constant amount of new coins is analogous to gold miners expending resources to add gold to circulation."*

Bitcoin was similar to gold in another way. It appealed to the anti-inflation, store-of-value investor types, the same people who bought gold. Only twenty-one million bitcoins would ever be created, which is zero inflation for eternity. Since money has value only if people think it has value, this store-of-value attribute was a brilliant move by Satoshi.

The cypherpunk community turned to the Bitcoin white paper and tried to find its flaws. They couldn't. It appeared he'd done it. The clouds parted. Their combined brainpower, applied over time, had found a simple and apparently flawless solution.

They'd fiddled with the figurative lock on the computer room for decades. No one thought they'd ever get in, but they kept trying. Then, suddenly, the door opened. These anarchists, hackers, Dungeons and Dragons enthusiasts, and self-proclaimed revolutionaries had been fighting for their vision of personal liberty with sticks and stones. They'd just acquired a lightsaber.

Before long, several hundred computers pointed their power at the Bitcoin blockchain. And it worked. Before long, the network had more computing power than all of Google's servers combined.

But more importantly, Bitcoin had opened Pandora's box. It had proved decentralization was an organizing principle that worked. Hypothetically, other things could be decentralized.

From the moment the price of bitcoin started rising, the world focused almost exclusively on the price and very little on the underlying philosophy of decentralization. And who could blame them? In its first two years, despite high volatility, bitcoin was up 10,000 percent, making its early adopters filthy rich.

As for Satoshi, no one knows if that pseudonym belongs to a man, a woman, or a group of people. We may never know, because despite being nominated for a Nobel Prize in 2016 and sitting on a stash of bitcoins worth billions, Satoshi vanished in 2012, never to be heard from again.

I remember reading an article about Bitcoin back then. I thought it sounded like total bullshit.

CHAPTER FOUR

CURRENTS

O n my first day at Acme, I travelled up the elevator to the twentieth floor and started my career at the new company. In an odd bit of timing, before being introduced to everyone individually, I'd be joining a previously scheduled meeting of the California leadership team with executives from Red State and New York. In most cases, I'll be referring to persons from Red State, California, and New York by those division names, rather than individual names. In the maze of organizational charts that is Acme, I worked day-to-day with California, reported to Red State, and feared New York.

Red State and I arrived at the conference room first and sat next to each other at one end of a long oval table. A few moments later, the rest of the group entered. They were talking about a project I was obviously not yet familiar with as they arranged themselves around the table. We were one chair short, so an executive assistant was summoned to get another chair from a nearby office. Finally, we got started.

"Hi, everyone, this is Dan Conway. We didn't want him to miss any of the fun, so he's going to join us today, even though he is brand new," Red State said.

Everyone chuckled. Standard corporate irony.

"Thank you, Red State," I said. "I'm glad to be here, and I look forward to spending time with each of you later." I settled into my seat. I was relieved not to have to say anything more.

The meeting was to discuss the California team's number-one priority, which it had failed to achieve after several years of effort: winning approval for Acme's widget factory in San Francisco. The city was the last major metropolitan area in Acme's footprint to not have a widget factory. Neighborhood activists were fighting the build. They didn't want the smoke stacks.

Once I processed what they were talking about, it was obvious to me why the California team hadn't been able to get it done. The San Francisco Board of Supervisors is famously feisty. This was a heavy lift. This didn't appear to be obvious to Red State. I found out later that in other regions, Acme entered markets like conquering heroes. Not so in San Francisco, though the company had given a ton of money to community groups, snuggled up to each supervisor, and made rounds of concessions at the behest of the board.

"It's been two years, and it doesn't seem like we are any closer," Red State said. "Are you guys going to be able to pull this off?"

One of the leaders of the California team was a senior executive I'll call Prince Charming. As the room turned toward him, I noticed he was wearing a gorgeous suit and a smirk. He had pale white skin and bright blue eyes. I soon became familiar with his endearing liberal arrogance. I also discovered that he was despised by the aw-shucks Red Staters and their allies in the middle-America divisions of the company.

"I feel like I'm on *The Price is Right* again," Prince Charming said.

Apparently that was an inside joke, because everyone other than Red State laughed.

"I'm seeing the mayor tomorrow at a reception. I'll talk to him. He's always more open to me after 8 p.m." Here he was, being grilled by Red State, and he found a way to make a joke. Again, everyone laughed, including me. I loved his irreverence.

Then he turned to me and said, "With Dan on board, we should be able to get it done, right, Dan?" As if the perfect messaging would get the board to vote for that factory. He was mocking Red State.

"Oh, yes, of course!" I said. I hoped I didn't appear to be playing along.

I did have a lot of experience getting land use projects approved in Northern California. As usual, my track record was frustratingly mixed. Earlier in my career, before Safeway, I worked for a firm that helped big box retailers. Once, when my boss was sick and couldn't make a meeting, I single-handedly won a new client project by giving an inspired presentation to a group of Home Depot executives.

But a few weeks later, during the next presentation with the same group, Flip Side appeared out of nowhere, his arms bulging with muscles as he squeezed my head. I lost my words for "excited about," "eager to start," and "looking forward to." The only phrase I could come up with was "lick my chops." I told them I'd lick my chops three times during my ten minutes. After the meeting, my boss told me to never, ever use that phrase again. I was shaken, because I'd never used the expression before and didn't even know what it alluded to at a literal level. Was "chops" the same as "loins"? Had I just told a group of executives that I was so excited to get started that I was going to suck my own dick?

"San Francisco believes it's different from Tulsa," Prince Charming continued. "We always knew it would take a while to get this done, but we're on the right track."

Left unsaid was the insinuation that Red State should know that by now.

Red State had what it wanted … Prince Charming on record, saying he could get it done.

I noticed how each side kept looking at the New York executives. They were positioned by the net, watching this prickly, passive-aggressive tennis match.

"Well, I guess the proof will be in the pudding," New York said. "Let's see how things develop. We will give you any support we can from our corner of the world."

The conversation moved on. As a palate cleanser, New York said something about the San Francisco Giants and how they'd like to steal a couple of their pitchers and bring them back to the Yankees. Not a funny joke, but a good opportunity to pivot beyond the Red State/California dynamic.

I'd spent the meeting trying to figure out the incentives of the people talking. The internal politics were clearly more important than the project we were there to discuss.

I'd soon have to engage with these people directly. I was a thirty-nine year old professional with a lot of experience, but the whole vibe of that meeting and the people there felt like the purest form of classical corporate dynamics I'd ever seen. It felt like I'd just stumbled into the production studio for a television show featuring old-school corporate sharks going at it. I was an extra on *Romper Room* next door who had mistakenly sat my manchild-self down at their table. I knew I had Imposter Syndrome, but I feared I was a *real-life imposter.*

After the meeting I wandered around the office, meeting my new co-workers. They would invariably say, "Oh, the new *Fourth Level.* Nice to meet you."

For the past hundred years, and still today, Acme has categorized employees by management levels, and it is everything. A person's level determines salary, vacation, bonus, and the respect they're afforded. Everyone's always asking: Is she Second Level? What's your plan to get to Third Level? Why the hell is he a Fifth Level? How much bonus does a Fourth Level get?

First Levels are the unmentionables. They are the ones who interact with the public: the customer service staff and administrative assistants. They earn a wage and don't normally expect to rise any further.

Second Levels are frontline managers. They do a lot of the day-to-day work of the company. Young, promising Second Levels can earn respect, because everyone knows they can rise up fast if the spotlight shines on them. They might become a fashionable pawn for an executive who wants to show they have a tremendous eye for talent.

The older Second Levels who have been in their positions for years are like forty-year-old minor league baseball players. It is highly unlikely that they're going to start hitting .400. Even if they went on a streak, there wouldn't be any scouts in the stands to see it. No one is paying attention to the chronic Second Levels.

Third Levels are Directors, and they have the real glow of management. In some parts of the company, Third Levels are in charge of hundreds of employees and are treated like legitimate big shots. I met a number of them at Acme training sessions in Atlanta and Houston. They had all the trappings of an old-school business person: handsome rings, beautiful ties, carefully worded language, and crushing handshakes.

Fourth Levels are the real managers in my division. This was my level. I was told that Second and Third Levels are supposed to be master implementers and excellent at their jobs, with the ability, of course, to be strategic. But Fourth Levels were something special and a step above. They had the ability to "move the organization" and "see a few miles ahead." Fourth Levels relish the opportunity to whiteboard the shit out of a problem in front of a big group, and can awe the crowd with their vision.

Fifth Level is where the real money flows. Big bonuses, huge options, mucho respect. Being a Fifth Level is like making partner at a law firm. Fifth Levels manage collections of teams. Each of them know the CEO, because they interview with him. If you have a Fifth Level on your side, you're swinging a big dick. This is where I wanted to be.

Sixth Levels are officers of the company and are treated like dangerous celebrities. There were about eighty Acme officers when I joined, roughly one for every five thousand employees. They are considered so precious that the company pays for them to fly into a special clinic and undergo a day-long executive physical. They're strapped into breathing and heart monitors to check their cardiovascular health. Their urine, blood, and feces are harvested for testing. A doctor with all the time in the world explains the findings and, I presume, recommends a diet to meet the specific needs of their feces.

Officers also receive a clothing allowance, as if they need it. They fly all over the world on a whim. They make so much money that the company strongly recommends that they have their money professionally managed and refers them to a financial advisor. After a few years, they have enough money to retire, if they want to. Few ever let go until their position is wrenched from their cold, dead hands.

At the top of the food chain are the seven CEO direct reports. Each is in charge of a kingdom, like in *Game of Thrones*. There were a number of disruptions on the small council during my time at the company. Following the banishment or beheading, that person's newly orphaned chain of command shook with downward cascading impacts. Divisions were ravaged and scavenged for talent. Projects were cancelled in midstream, simply because they no longer had an executive sponsor.

Another set of constituents has to be recognized, because they make everything so much more difficult, especially during critical campaigns: the Machines—Acme's computerized systems, reports, automated processes, and other instruments of centralized control. The Machines are every employee's first and continuing adversary.

The Machines enforce the rules at Acme. They are so bloated and unmanageable that no one, not even someone high up on the chain, can change them without screwing up the whole organization.

The Machines practice lifelike malevolence against human beings. They crash expense reports when they are nearly complete, losing all of your work. They require automated trainings on Sunday mornings due to glitches in the system. They generate bot-like emails demanding reports on your interactions with computer systems you didn't even know you had access to.

The engineers who created the original machines are long dead, but the Machines live on, spawning and growing to infect each and every action an employee takes at Acme, from filing for mileage reimbursement to building access code certification, disaster readiness location verification, daily time tracking, and registration for maternity leave via the X89 system. God help those booking travel through the People Matter! Portal.

CHAPTER FIVE

COFFEE AND CONFUSION

I worked feverishly to gain a foothold. The Machines put up a stiff resistance. At the same time that I was trying to establish credibility with my team and show strategic insights to the big shots in California, Red State, and New York, I had the mounting number of email chains I'd been added to. I was trying to sign up for health insurance, enroll in the employee giving campaign, and complete a mountain of required online training courses. The computers crashed constantly, at all the wrong times.

I had a full head of steam driven by fear and ambition. When I fully grasped the importance of the levels of management, two thoughts came to mind. First and most importantly, *Holy shit, I hope I can do what is required of a Fourth Level.* And secondly, *How do I get to Fifth Level?* That's where the real money was made and where I'd one day earn the salary I was (not) promised.

I worked my ass off. I've never been an outstanding sleeper, so once convinced I wasn't going to fall back asleep, I'd get up early, sometimes at four. I'd drive to BART, get on a train like a zombie and arrive in downtown San Francisco when even the financial types on an East Coast schedule were just getting started.

Driven by a feeling that I was ahead of the game, I'd make myself a strong cup of coffee in the corporate kitchen and settle in for two or three hours of work before anyone arrived. I'd already have an inbox full of emails from Red State and New York. to deal with. I couldn't respond to all of them, so I had to quickly figure out which ones needed my attention. Red State was particularly aggressive in asking my opinion on issues that I'd barely grasped or was not yet familiar with. *Ok*, I told myself. *This is the big leagues, so suck it up and get it done.*

There were numerous weekly calls with large regional teams comprised of people like me all over the country. Some were pure fluff and could be blown off, like Widget Wednesdays!, an internal training call that no one joined, but I didn't know that yet. There were impromptu calls foisted onto my schedule by Red State and New York to discuss new ideas, projects, and initiatives dreamed up by ambitious executives who had bright ideas for California. I was often the only California representative invited to attend and was charged with sharing the "good news" about our assignments with the executives down the hall.

When normal business hours began at 9:00 a.m., I'd walk down the hall to one or more offices and explain to them what I (we?) had been asked to do. They frequently didn't understand the strategy. Sometimes I didn't fully understand it, either. In my dialogue with Red State, I hadn't asked enough questions. In fairness to me, when I did ask questions, Red State implied I was either too stupid to understand what was being asked or that I had caught the California disease of defying central authority.

Since most of the people with these good ideas were higher than me on the chain, I couldn't simply ignore them. The incentives of the system encouraged them to offer more ideas. They were simply hunting for their own credit in the corporate structure we were all operating in.

Red State was constantly asking me, "Do they have the votes?" in reference to our California lobbyist's attempt to pass legislation beneficial to the company. At first, I shared my thoughts candidly. But I found that Red State used this sensitive information as a weapon, making me look like a careless gossip at best and a turncoat at worst. One of my new co-workers in California spelled it out for me, though I was already getting the picture. "You need to be very careful about what you tell Red State, or else people here will shut you out."

I also had to protect Red State. California had a special relationship with New York. After I told my California workmates about the projects Red State asked us to pursue, they would backchannel to New York. The chronic complaint was that Red State wanted red-state strategies in blue-state California. California used my relayed requests to make Red State look like ham-fisted yokels. This would get me in trouble with Red State who, after being questioned and castigated by New York, would come to the conclusion that I'd fucked up describing the original direction. Or maybe that I was too stupid to understand it in the first place.

To be honest, sometimes I was slow on the uptake. But on many occasions, I felt I was being handed a half-baked idea fired off on a whim, of roughly the same quality as gibberish jotted down when waking from a dream.

In the afternoons, in between lunch, conference calls, and in-person meetings, I drank a lot of coffee. I needed to be juiced to keep up with the emails and projects. My own team was only marginally helpful.

I was not a particularly skilled manager.

Acme believed in the cult of the leader. I'd done good work in my career, but if I was honest with myself, I never felt comfortable acting as a leader. But that was the only path I saw to move up and make more money. I had also had mostly negative experiences working with so-called leaders, who usually had as many blind spots as I did. I felt most comfortable when I was doing the actual work, forgetting for a moment about having to defend my status in the chain of command.

Now that I was at my limits trying to establish myself on so many fronts, my confidence flagged. To build morale and show off my generosity, I treated my whole team to lunch one day at a high-end taqueria a few blocks away. Normally, lunch was my critical time to recharge, an urgent hour-long break from the storm of demands. I'd go off on my own, pull up a chair at the dingy Thai food place on Kearney Street, and inhale green curry with pork and the sports page.

I felt my battery blinking red at this team lunch. Two old hats told a long story about times past. They shot each other a look when I asked for the definition of a well-known widget acronym. Since I was the boss, everyone was paying close attention whenever I spoke. It made me uncomfortable. Every time I talked, little bits of taco shell flew from my mouth at my team. I was the only one who couldn't control this talking-while-eating thing. Flip Side had apparently worked his way into my central nervous system.

I was able to weed out a few people who were jaded, ineffective, and toxic. It took enormous effort. The Machines required performance to be graded on a long list of nonsensical criteria, a soup of mumbo-jumbo best practices in vogue over the past forty years. The criteria had solidified in the

Machines like fossils in stone, cholesterol in arteries. I had to demonstrate underperformance by rating employees according to categories like "Ability to Inspire through Program Management" and "Willingness to Lead through Teamwork." I was looking for the field that asked, "Is this Person a Useless Asshole?" Because when you work with someone day in and day out, you know.

On the other end of the staffing life cycle, the Machines required Machiavellian and outdated public job postings that made us look like we were searching for cold-blooded killers. At a time when Acme was doubling down on smiley faces, perky hashtags and impossibly happy people in their TV ads, the job description listed a preference for candidates who could "influence through persuasion tactics," and "achieve policy objectives by directing public sentiment." In other words, if you were one of the operatives in *The Manchurian Candidate,* hit me up!

The systems all seemed so absurd and a waste of everyone's time. I'd experienced bureaucracy and bullshit at past jobs, of course. All those things were concentrated and magnified at Acme.

Since Acme was one of the oldest companies in the Fortune 500, it made sense that these systems were entrenched. It felt like the end-stage of a dystopian corporate nightmare path many large companies might follow as they aged over the decades. I honestly didn't give it too much thought other than constantly thinking, *What a hassle.* If I was ever going to escape, I first needed to survive and ultimately climb this ladder, no matter how badly it was shaking.

CHAPTER SIX

ETHEREUM, A NEW KIND OF MACHINE

I n his famous 1937 book *The Modern Firm*, economist Ronald Coase Noah explains why corporations have run the world economy for so long. They allow contracts to be settled, and they make it possible for people to work together to get things done. By and large, people have been working under this template for generations. The litany of complaints at your local watering hole are the bedrock of the corporation: chains of command, bureaucracy, and a culture that values polished professionals with similar temperaments and few rough edges.

In his book *Sapiens: A Brief History of Humankind*, Yuval Noah Harari points out that man is built to work together, to some degree. But Harari's work doesn't study how deep or long-term this cooperation is intended to be.

I'm skeptical that early humans would recognize today's version of cooperation in the modern corporation. Take a group of prehistoric men on a deer hunt. Put them in chairs all day long and instruct them to send each other carefully typed messages through a glowing screen. Inform them that their day will be punctuated by brief spurts of rubbing up against each other's insecurities and molesting each other's blind spots across a round table down the hall, according to a hierarchy and rules enforced by the Machines and corporate culture. That's not what they signed up for.

Of course, it's not always that bad for everyone. But the stats show that for many of us, it is. According to a 2016 Society for Human Resource Management study, fewer than one-third of employees are very satisfied with the teamwork at their companies. We've become so used to the misery of modern work that we accept it like a sliver deep in our heel.

Despite low levels of job satisfaction, most economists would say the firm remains the best way to organize humans for work. Which reminds me of what Winston Churchill said about modern government: "Democracy is the worst form of government, except for all of the others." The same could have been said of the modern firm. Until it wasn't.

While I was struggling to master the corporate world, which had always eluded me, a young genius named Vitalik Buterin was creating Ethereum. More on Vitalik later.

Ethereum is a "Turing complete blockchain," which means it can be programmed to do anything. Whereas Bitcoin has the functionality of a calculator and can transact digital money, Ethereum has the functionality of a computer and is a trustless—thus, supremely trustworthy —platform to transact any type of business.

To understand this, you need to think of Ethereum not as a way to buy coffee with digital money but as a computer that can be accessed with the cryptocurrency, ether (ETH).

The role of trust is a big deal in blockchain philosophy. Corporations do business by pooling resources and establishing trust with their customers, employees, and partners. As I mentioned, up until now, scaling trust was an expensive undertaking that required centralization in the form of compliance applications, organizational charts, and homogeneous corporate cultures.

The computer systems that comprise the Machines at Acme are basically trust engines. They hum along at all hours demanding adherence to corporate rules for workplace behavior, expense reports, travel guidelines, salary increases, and a million other things. These reports provide trust to managers to verify that their departments are creating economic value, as promised.

Ethereum's killer app is the smart contract, an unalterable, ironclad agreement between two or more parties that is validated by the blockchain. If something happens at point X, the blockchain enforces the contracted action at point Y. The people whose computers are "mining blocks" (anyone who wants to) are rewarded with a small amount of ETH for validating these transactions on the blockchain. This is the engine that keeps Ethereum running without any central control or funding.

As a fully functional third-party ledger, Ethereum has the potential, as it matures, to run corporate alternatives as decentralized entities. These decentralized corporations running on a blockchain wouldn't need, or even allow, centralized control. This could theoretically allow people to work without becoming employees of a firm or having to play by its rules.

This would allow everyone, including those deemed less desirable in today's economy, to earn a living by contributing to projects that suit them. An elderly lady with no corporate experience but a lot of intellectual curiosity could help design a decentralized recipe-sharing application just by plugging into the blockchain. An ex-con could jump in and contribute to a decentralized government accounting audit. An insecure man like myself could write content for a public relations campaign without having to fake confidence. We'd all be rewarded with ether or other cryptocurrency, which could be converted to dollars.

It sounds touchy-feely, a little scary, and also too good to be true. We aren't there yet, by a long shot. But a lot of future-looking, smart people believe it is coming.

Naval Ravikant is CEO of AngelList. He is one of the best at explaining how the blockchain-based Internet could be the heart of a new, decentralized economy. Why does Ravikant think this is more likely to happen now, years after the migration to the gig economy and independent contractors is underway? Blockchains powered by cryptocurrency. He says, "The Internet evolved media from physical to digital, from paid to free, from editorial to social. Next up: from corporate to ownerless."

The gig economy provides some measure of freedom, but it still requires people to play by the corporate rules, like Google's army of contractors, or hand over a disproportionate cut to its market maker, like Uber and Airbnb. In the gig economy, workers more or less still need to know the right people, laugh at the right jokes, and have the right credentials.

On this open Internet, blockchains would allow independent agents to compete on an even playing field. They would choose when they want to work in communion with those they select, for a price they set. The cartels who now make the rules and are rich enough to own the trust machines would no longer have a stranglehold on the economy.

As Ravikant explains, this would be groundbreaking economic freedom. He says, "Blockchains are a new invention that allow meritorious participants in an open network to govern without a ruler."

The results would be transformative, not just for individuals but for business as we know it. He says, "An economy run by markets/blockchains instead of middlemen/authorities would make our current society look like a communist bureaucracy."

Techcrunch summed up the revolutionary potential of Ethereum in the article "Business in the Age of Ethereum": "Blockchain technology provides a platform for people to work together with the persistence and stability of an organization but without the hierarchy."

In an article titled "Disrupting the Trust Business," *The Economist* placed this invention in its historical context: "If double-entry bookkeeping freed accounting from the merchant's head, the blockchain frees it from the confines of an organisation." Eventually, over time, as *The Economist* asserts, "Some companies could be no more than a bundle of smart contracts, forming true virtual firms that live only on a blockchain."

CHAPTER SEVEN

TAKING THE EDGE OFF

I t was clear that this job was more difficult than I'd imagined it would be. I was determined to make it work. The stakes were obviously high, considering the three souls Eileen and I were raising. So I was happy to blow off steam when I could.

On the drinking front, thankfully, our peer group at this time—friends from school and the neighborhood—were enjoying heavy alcohol consumption. I didn't usually stand out. We'd all been thrown together, and we had a lot in common. We showed up at the same places, like Little Gym, Small Heathens' Drumming Class at the rec center, and the big slide at Coyote Point. It was easy to meet up at Celia's for a big margarita dinner. It was a lot of fun.

I'd go to Beverages and More on two-cent Tuesdays and load up on wine, using the sale as an excuse to buy a big stash. Eileen constantly asked if I was drinking a normal amount, and I'd feed her a steady stream of bullshit, assuring her that I was.

Eileen and I would sometimes have margaritas together. That was fun. I'd make mine "authentic" with just tequila and a splash of lime and hers "normal" with a lot of sweetener. We talked about having a two-person 80s dance party in the kitchen after the kids were asleep, but we rarely found the time.

I was finding my pleasure from the booze, rather than my family. With my hectic work schedule, answering emails late into the night, and having to care for the kids during every free moment, I relied on the alcohol to accelerate my decompression. Eileen was as busy as I was. We never had time to talk, and I could never tell what was on her mind. It was clear we were drifting apart, but that seemed less important than keeping everything running.

I had also been dealing with another major stressor involving my sister, Maureen.

Maureen was sixteen years older than me. She'd always been the most unabashedly Conway-like among us. Once, at her daughter Mary's post-softball game gathering at Round Table Pizza, La Bamba played on the jukebox. That was Maureen's favorite song, so she jumped up on the table and sang the whole thing, becoming an instant legend. To be clear, no alcohol was involved.

When each of my children was born, Maureen stayed in the hospital waiting room no matter how long it took, despite any other obligations. She loved underdogs. She was always drawn to the quietest people at any party. She wanted them to have some fun. Later, she might flash her boobs. Once I mooned a man in the park who was filming me because my dog was off-leash. I briefly feared I'd be arrested for a sex crime. I realized I'd been channeling Maureen.

She called me one day, about a year before I started at Acme. "Hi, honey," she said. "I just wanted to tell you, they think I have leukemia."

A few weeks before, at her annual St. Paddy's Day party, I had noticed she wasn't laughing much. Normally, like the rest of us, she'd be butchering the lyrics of Irish folk songs and relishing stories of our grandmother, Nana, who had a heart of gold but would push the kids with her cane and tell them to "keep still" if they were too loud.

Maureen found blood in her urine. Tests indicated it was a leukemia-related tumor.

"The doctors tell me they can knock out the tumor with radiation, but they also need to treat the underlying leukemia. I'm going to UCSF tomorrow. It's a weird type, apparently."

When my dad was sick with terminal lung cancer years before, I practically got a Ph.D. in cancer via the Internet. Since then, I'd been closely tracking anyone on my Facebook feed who was dealing with cancer. A "weird" type was obviously what you didn't want to hear.

"Don't worry, it's going to be all right," I said. "UCSF is one of the best hospitals in the world, and I'm sure they have all sorts of amazing treatments." It's interesting how quickly I could dish out platitudes with conviction while my brain was screaming, "This is BAD!"

As time went on, we became more concerned with each update. The cancer was uncontrolled, strange, vibrant. There was a troubling lilt in the doctors' voices when they talked about Maureen's condition.

In the meantime, as is always the case, I needed to make a living. So I'd go from taking a call about Maureen's status on the busy sidewalk on Montgomery Street, where I didn't have to worry about getting emotional, to going back upstairs to send cogent-sounding emails, plan meeting agendas, and edit press releases.

I started to feel that I was being tamed, that my family was being tamed. I was struggling at work. And a core member of my family was suffering and might die. The cold, hard world was turning on me and my family. All my thoughts of early retirement were gone, and I just wanted to survive. Of course, I wouldn't acknowledge that I was throwing booze on this dumpster fire, hoping it would go out.

I kept plugging along. After a long day at work, I'd pull up in front of our house and brace myself for kid duty. I'd paint a smile on my face, grit my teeth and get through dinner, cleanup, and baths. I loved them, but with the constant demands to assemble toys, make dinner, and clean up messes, I didn't have any time alone to unwind. I was ashamed that I felt this way.

After we returned from a one-week vacation to Russian River, where we'd spent each day playing catch, building sand castles, and making blackberry pies, I stayed in the BART parking lot for a few moments to have a cry. I knew I wasn't going to be as present for my kids, now that the pressures of real life had returned. I knew I wasn't being a good dad.

At night, I'd get back on email from nine p.m. until midnight, and sometimes until one or two a.m. I was determined to succeed at this job, and that meant learning everything I could and answering as many emails as possible. No matter how hard I tried, there seemed to be more incoming than I could deal with.

I chalked up some wins on projects that didn't require managing the rift between Red State and California. Some California team members dropped by to say, "Great job." Red State said, "Good job, and it's about time California did something right." I was recognized, and it felt good.

My reward was an email up the chain. The prize for doing something good at Acme was a positive note from a supervisor that cascaded gloriously out of the bowels of the day-to-day work, to the warmth and brightness of the thirty-first floor of the Red State skyscraper. It was a way for everyone in the chain of command to associate themselves with awesome work and take a little bit of credit for themselves. It was amazing to see how high these emails could go. On occasion, they'd go all the way to the CEO and the board of directors. At some point, there would be no one more senior to send it to, leaving only Jesus Christ or Dick Cheney to say, "Great work."

If the project being applauded involved a buzzword in fashion at the time, you could win a cascading, upwardly mobile email for an achievement so trivial it was laughable. Sharp-eyed managers would spot the connection and launch the note vertically before anyone beat them to the punch. They'd write something like, *Mary, this is a great example of leveraging synergies with NGOs ... thought you should see our work here.* And just like that, out of nowhere, that note with your original email would skyrocket to the powers that be, one manager at a time.

On one occasion, I wrote an email to my supervisor with a good deal of necessary background information. It was simply an explanation of something that needed explaining, nothing extraordinary. To my great shock and pleasure, this note was deemed "storytelling." Unbeknownst to me, a traveling motivational speaker had recently impressed the Red State executives with the need for more storytelling. No one knew what that meant, but apparently I was very skilled at it. My note exploded vertically, and I was momentarily and gloriously celebrated as one of Acme's very own top-notch storytellers by a number of senior vice presidents I recognized from their scripted town hall webcasts.

The herd mentality of the corporate culture grated on me. One executive or another was always promoting a new process or snappy best practice. Employees were expected to rally around these ideas with exclamation points and big smiles.

Flip Side was now running around like never before, screwing up most of the work-related words out of my mouth. I turned to humor for stress relief. When my jokes landed, it made me feel like I was at least good at something.

I'd seen other Californians with a good sense of humor thread that needle, knowing when to turn it up or down, never erring from an approved range. But that wasn't me. I'd go for broke to get the laugh, going right beyond the line of appropriate. Once, during a particularly serious discussion when we were all twisted up figuring out how Acme could influence San Diego Neighborhood Councils with our philanthropic efforts and other corporate AstroTurf strategies, I said with a straight face, "I think it's time we consider buying a neighborhood council."

There was a pause, and then everyone burst into laughter, everyone except the silent marshals from Red State. I received a chilling email to "watch my humor."

There was a beautiful electric display in my office that showed thousands of colorful dots connected by a bird's nest of wires. It was supposed to show the great power and complexity of Acme's operations on the Internet. It had been commissioned by one of my predecessors at a time when the company was desperately trying to prove it was a top-notch tech company.

I'd use it as a prop to break the ice when candidates came in for job interviews. After greeting them warmly, I'd escort them to my office and direct them to the display.

"This is Acme's Internet presence. If I hear of a transmission problem, I can go to this display and identify a *possible issue*," I'd explain. "It's definitely not foolproof, but more often than not, there is a trunk line that can be rerouted, and we can deal with it *very deliberately*."

We'd both continue staring at the display. Every single time, the candidate would express their awe with complete sincerity, matching my deep reflection and focus. Either they actually believed I could scan the Internet and perform maintenance, or they thought I was crazy but decided to humor me so that I'd hire them. Finally, I'd tell them I was kidding and explode into borderline inappropriate laughter, the kind that makes me extremely unattractive when I'm watching YouTube prank videos, according to my wife.

I'd also ask candidates if they'd like a glass of water. If they said yes, I'd disappear into the kitchen and bring back a square black container that was clearly a small flower vase. The person would always take it and would never indicate that drinking water out of a pot during an interview was unusual. I couldn't look at the water without losing it, so I completely blocked it out. I would've been mortified if someone actually drank from it, but they never did.

Aside from these (I hope) harmless jokes, I was extremely nice to the people who came in looking for a job. One type of candidate frightened me: those who were out of work with long, impressive resumes, high-powered grad school credentials, and probably big mortgages. Anyone over forty practically begged me to hire them for Second or Third Level jobs. What had happened to these people, I wondered? They'd been thrown off whatever professional vessel they'd been riding to retirement.

CHAPTER EIGHT

THIS IS BAD

Maureen kept getting worse. She needed a bone marrow transplant to live. I have three siblings, including Maureen. After donor testing, we were all matches—except Maureen, who only partially matched each of us. She proceeded with a bone marrow transplant from a stranger off the registry who was as genetically close as they could find.

Following a bone marrow transplant, recipients require round-the-clock monitoring and care with complicated, high-stakes drug administration. I honestly don't know how anyone without a big family or other substantial support network manages. Luckily, we come from a large, tight-knit family, and everyone pitched in to help. We put together a detailed care schedule. I was on duty with my brother, sister, mother, cousins, Maureen's partner, her kids, and close friends.

The transplant halfway took. Her body didn't reject it, but her stomach became so inflamed, she couldn't eat. Every week brought new crises.

I'd visit her at the recovery center after work. Before walking through the lobby with the antiseptic smell, I'd visit the liquor store in the strip mall next door. I'd buy a flask of vodka and pour it into a half bottle of orange juice.

I didn't feel like I was doing something bad. In my mind, I was simply using the booze to access the best part of my family and myself. The part that scoffs at convention and goes for broke. The part that told Maureen it was a good idea to sneak onto Hank Williams Jr.'s tour bus after a concert in 1987. I told myself that booze wasn't the endgame but a vehicle to let it all hang out, to be a Conway.

Eileen was sorry she had let me start drinking, though of course she had no power to stop me. One night, after I started at Acme, seemingly out of the blue, she told me she thought I had a problem. I couldn't believe what I was hearing. I asked her what on earth she was referring to. I was usually the drunkest person at any party we attended. I had at least three drinks every night from the moment I took that first sip of wine. But I didn't end up in a Mexican jail, get a DUI, or show up drunk for work.

She calmly said, "You've changed," and walked upstairs to bed.

That scared me. I couldn't deny that this was starting to sound like the preamble to serious marital problems, perhaps even a divorce. But with my addiction growing, my career crumbling, and my sister dying, I wasn't prepared to do anything about it.

Now that I was fully ensconced in my drinking life, wine and chewing tobacco were important components of my nightly routine as I plowed through emails. Also strong Manhattans and margaritas, depending on the season. I'm like a lot of alcoholics and drug addicts who never get tired after taking substances, even sedatives. Anything that made me feel different, stimulant or depressant, energized me. With a few drinks in me, I had more stamina to keep pulling up the next email.

It goes without saying that once I started drinking, exercise became something other people did. I didn't have the time. And my sleep wasn't getting any better, so I talked to my doctor about Ambien. I got a prescription and started using it nearly every night. I slept like a rock, but I didn't dream, which made me a little edgy. Maybe my lower back pain was keeping me out of REM sleep. I got a prescription for Vicodin and started taking one before bed and also when I needed a pick-me-up.

The emails kept coming in at all hours—demands from Red State, reporting requirements from the Machines. One early morning, after a late night, I was still groggy and drove into the back of a SamTrans bus. It barely moved, but my car was totaled. The driver claimed to be injured and had to be taken out on a stretcher. I hoped she hated her job, and I'd given her the perfect out.

If I had them, I'd take two Vicodin before extended play sessions with the kids. Sometimes we'd all be driving down El Camino to one event or another, and Eileen would ask why I was driving so slowly. Sure enough, I was going twenty in a thirty-five. So I'd hit the gas and we'd fly forward, exceeding the speed limit as I lost myself in the flow of substances running through my brain.

***

The only thing intending to grow more bloated than my face was Acme, which announced a $12 billion acquisition of Globex in early 2011.

This was full-scale war. All of the troops were being activated. The generals on our call were talking louder than normal, laying it on the line, telling us how important this was for the company.

I knew I'd have a big role in this effort and was excited to get started. The perpetually complicated dynamics between California and Red State seemed surmountable, since we'd all be fully aligned and working like hell to get this merger approved. That weekend, I spent a lot of time at the library gathering my thoughts. I drew up the beginnings of a plan that I thought would get us off to the right start in California. This acquisition might be my path to success.

Then Red State emailed to tell me I wouldn't be working on Globex. They said I had too much on my plate with the San Francisco widget factory project. This was devastating news, to say the least. It was like being relieved of command before D-Day. I would be the only public relations lead in the country not working on the acquisition.

Leadership at Acme made a big point of referring to us as a family, a tribe bound by something greater than the bottom line, though that thing was never identified. If you believe that, you must have come from a pretty fucked-up family.

As an ostracized member of that family, I now went through the embarrassing process of declining to participate in acquisition-related conference calls and meetings that I'd been invited to, explaining over and over again that I wasn't working on that project. But my team was working full steam ahead on it, and I was still their manager. Awkward. And devastating. It was like being forced to wear a "dead meat" sign around the office.

Going to work was hell. I hated the people in Red State with a cold heat. I dreamt of all of the things I'd like to tell them and their aw-shucks attitude as they continued to insert shivs into my guts.

The combination of booze, Vicodin, and Ambien at night was making me foggy during the day, paranoid during moments of contemplation, and overall at least twenty percent dopier than I already was. But in my heart of hearts, I pinned all of my problems on those miserable bastards in Red State.

I started furiously looking for jobs and had a few interviews. I came off as a desperate, shattered man with bloodshot eyes. They'd be sure to get back to me if anything else opened up. My ability to fake it during interviews no longer worked.

Home was anything but a sanctuary. As I mentioned, Eileen wasn't happy with me due to the drinking and my overall miserable disposition. Even friends weren't excited to see me. When I spilled a glass of red wine on a friend's shirt at a Friday night get-together at our house, he said, "Damnit, Dan, you have to be careful." I'd spilled a glass of wine on his couch the previous Friday. I made a note to avoid that asshole in the future.

I needed more relief, and I had an idea where I could find it. The Vicodin was great, but it ran out too quickly. I needed more Vicodin, because it really calmed me down and gave me some peace. My body had already been breached by addiction. This was just one more step.

A few years prior, I'd read a story in the *San Francisco Chronicle* about a place called Pill Hill in the Tenderloin District, a fifteen-minute walk from my office in the Financial District. I remembered the story focusing on the scourge of this place and how it was like a food court for drugs. People would walk by, get what they needed and go about their business. Very bad stuff. I thought I'd check it out.

The Tenderloin was a dystopian hell. It had been a drug-infested den for more than sixty years, a home for desperate, impoverished lost souls. As I walked down Seventh Street in my suit, I spied many horrors: people lying in their own vomit with matted hair and no shoes, small children yelling "Fuck you" at one another while playing in traffic, and grizzled, zombie-like humans sitting on the sidewalk, some in wheelchairs, staring vacantly into the distance. Each retail storefront was protected with heavy bars. Sirens crashed as police cruisers raced by.

There was so much malfeasance happening in the Tenderloin that the SFPD placed an entire station in the middle of the neighborhood. Ultimately, nothing ever seemed to change the mood of the place, not the shiny happy people from Twitter's new headquarters down the street or the multitude of recovery and rehab charities in the area.

I had a feeling I was about to do something very bad. It's the same feeling I had in third grade when I stole a candy bar from Safeway. I didn't remember having that feeling as an adult. *This is what it feels like to be a criminal*, I thought. It was a scene from a movie, certainly not my life. But there was Flip Side on my shoulder, who kept whispering how good I'd feel after taking a few Vics. I knew he was right.

I walked for about fifteen minutes, which is all you need to see the whole neighborhood, then I doubled back. I figured the guy in the leather jacket near the liquor store might be able to help me out. He was muscular and peppy. His head darted from side to side.

As I walked by, I asked, "Do you have any Vics?"

He looked at me and said, "Yeah, what do you need?"

He had five, and they were five dollars each. I said Ok and walked a little further. I looked around, didn't see any cops and took out my wallet.

He said, "Shit, man, get your money around the corner, then give it to my partner." His head nodded toward a younger guy in an impeccably white t-shirt.

I expected to be hauled off to jail in the next few moments, my life in tatters. But I really wanted those Vics. I did as I was told. The young guy took my money. The other guy said, "Wait a minute."

I walked in the vicinity for a moment, looking around at the storefronts. Then he walked toward me and handed me the pills and calmly took off in the other direction. He'd given me four Vics, which was not the deal, but good enough.

I ducked into a heavily secured liquor store, bought a water, and took two pills before exiting. Then I headed back to work and completed my day as if nothing had happened.

I'd just committed a felony. If I was arrested, I'd lose my job and probably my marriage and family. In addition, I'd have a hard time finding another job, because corporations aren't fond of hiring convicted felons to white-collar management positions.

But I had my Vics.

I swore I'd never go back to Pill Hill. Then, when my monthly prescription ran out, I'd find myself walking in that direction and repeating the same scene from *The Wire*, over and over again. But it never became routine, because nothing is easy when you're a junkie looking for dope.

Everyone was always trying to rip me off. They'd say the pills were Vics, but sometimes they sold me Tylenol, blood pressure medication, or fakes. Other times, they didn't have Vics, but they had OxyContin, a more powerful opiate I swore I'd never take. Once I started buying Oxys, I was up for any pill that was available: morphine, narcos, Percocet, etc. I could identify every opiate from its color, markings, and shape. Being able to identify a variety of pills was the only way I ever became street smart. The only one I didn't take was heroin.

One time a sick-looking old man in a wheelchair sold me some pills. When I got back to the office, I noticed they were covered in a red substance, which I assumed was blood. I threw them out, of course. Actually, I didn't. I flash-rinsed them under cold water, just a little, so that the pill wouldn't dissolve down the drain. After that, I was certain I had AIDS.

I never intended to keep going to Pill Hill long-term, but I could never find the right time to quit. My biggest fear was getting busted, since there were cop cars everywhere. I never saw an undercover cop bust someone, but I knew it was a threat, because the drug dealers were on constant lookout. Sometimes they told me it was "too hot" and brushed me off.

About half the time, drug dealers assumed I was the heat and refused to sell me anything.

"Nice try, cop," they'd say. I was a pretty sad-looking cop. With my sloppy computer bag slung over my shoulder and shaggy receding hairline, I'd clearly gone deep undercover.

Finally, I realized it was time to make a change. I needed to find a dedicated drug dealer. So that's what I did. I asked for a guy's number so that I could call him and order my drugs. I wouldn't give him my number, of course, since this was a company device with all sorts of monitoring software. I needed to be careful. So I'd call him from the payphone at the Montgomery BART station. I figured if any co-workers saw me, they'd assume I was having an affair, which seemed all right at the time.

My guy's name was James, and he looked about sixty, but he was probably much younger. He wasn't a high-end dealer, just another junkie from the streets who sold pills on the side. He had a wife who was younger and sharper than him. I believe I was the most precious, detail-focused pussy of a client he'd ever had, and it bugged him. He spoke street and I spoke middle manager, which made our time on the phone difficult and frustrating for both of us. A typical interaction went something like this:

"Hello, James?"

"Yeah, motherfucker?"

"It's Calvin." I used a pseudonym. "Do you have any Vics?"

"I gots some, but you be trippin' ifer down the way,"

"Excuse me, can you please repeat that? Did you say you have some Vics, and I can buy some?"

"That's what I said, man. Yo, this isn't the ones I been sayin' 'bout, so then you come and give it to me round Bush."

"Ok, are you indicating that you'd like to meet on Bush Street? I can be there at either two or three-thirty. Do either of those times work for you?"

"Man… I sick. I see you there then 'bout the time. Yo, don't be callin', I be sleepin'."

"Ok, then, I'll see you at two p.m. at that corner, does that work for you?"

CLICK.

Sometimes I'd meet him in the elevator at the BART station at Civic Station. Sometimes I'd meet him at a cafe in lower Pacific Heights. Once I met him at the McDonald's a few doors down from my office on Market Street. A few times I met him at the Carl's Jr. near City Hall. And that's where I met him the night of the widget factory vote.

Despite my new drug addiction, I was somehow still able to keep my head above water at work. I was feeling pretty good when the supervisors voted to approve the widget factory. That set off a frantic flurry of emails up the chain as each subgroup that contributed to the win crafted their team-spirity note, carving out their credit. I got my share, which was good since I wasn't a part of the much more important Globex deal. I felt particularly content because I'd pounded an OxyContin right before going through City Hall security.

CHAPTER NINE

A NOT-SO-INNOCENT
BYSTANDER

U nfortunately for the team working on Globex, that project was not going well. The merger was effectively killed by the State Department. There weren't a lot of happy campers in Red State. I was relieved since I wasn't officially part of this mess.

The traveling officers' visit is every Acme region's least-favorite ritual. It requires division staff to put on a dog and pony show for a collection of ancient Acme warriors, some of whom are close to death and others who've recently passed, but still enjoy the trip. They'd congratulate us on an outstanding year, regardless of whether they knew what year it was. Sometimes they actually forgot where they were. One officer, who talked mostly about golf and drank mostly Scotch, fell asleep two years in a row.

Following the Globex deal collapse, the traveling ancient officer visit would be much different, and it didn't sound good. All of our assistants received a curt message to hold February seventh and eighth open and to cancel all other meetings on those days. That's a message an officer's assistant was born to deliver. They listed three people who would give presentations, and I was one of them. This definitely wasn't the usual missive from the memory unit.

The company was in a foul mood about the Globex deal and opposition to it in California. We'd heard grumblings and jokes too close to the bone about how California "let this one get away." Of course, I personally couldn't be blamed for losing the World Series, since I was sent to the minors before Game One. And that was my dilemma. What was I supposed to do, remind everyone, "I wasn't even smart enough to be a part of the team, so you can't blame me!"

The ancient officers had been left home, and in their place were a number of sharp executives prepared to deliver a beating.

Sterling would be the lead voice for this group. He was a hybrid New York/Red State player and one of the most senior people in our division. He was the smoothest, most elegant executive I'd ever seen. He had a deep, Godfather-like voice that made you lean in closer. His eyes were moist and empathetic. Everything he said was strategy, and it was the real deal. He was practically created to thrive in corporate America. He was a beautiful man. If a movie was made about this situation, Sterling would play himself, because no actor could capture his pristine gravitas. Let me be even more clear. If I were forced at gunpoint to make love to a seventy-year-old-man, Sterling and I would be in the penthouse suite on Park Avenue, sipping champagne in bed.

Representing California was Prince Charming. The more I worked with him, the more impressed I was at his ability to endure in this chaotic environment. He never ceded a point, never portrayed weakness. He had a survivor's ability to curate information and use it to his advantage. A worthy adversary, to say the least.

I was also there.

I wanted to make sure I had a lot of energy at this meeting, since I was perpetually exhausted. I borrowed an Adderall from a friend who had a prescription. Adderall is speed. It helps people with ADD focus, but it also provides unlimited manic energy to anyone who consumes it.

The meeting was meant to be a slaughter. You could tell from the somber looks on the faces of the execution squad when they came in. Some of our perennial adversaries betrayed their hidden glee with bursts of pure laughter as they picked over muffins before the meeting began.

After Prince Charming gave a level-setting deck reviewing the California team's collective accomplishments, I was up. I knew what this situation called for: adrenaline. I was scared but chose to mask it with an extremely assertive approach. I tapped the same well of energy that allowed me to pitch the press with abandon, fully committing to the sale. I would be the alpha male of this presentation, motherfuckers. The Adderall was a big help.

The thesis of my presentation was that implementation was key, not strategy. First I reviewed all of the work my team had accomplished. In my mind, none of those things would've happened if we had sat around in meetings all day talking pretty and congratulating ourselves. In other words, all of the fancy thinking and clever-sounding emails were not nearly as important as securing press, building allies, getting real shit done outside of the internal Acme echo chamber.

I believed all of this, completely. We spent much more time talking to ourselves and making ourselves feel smart than we did on the actual work. But this was the exact wrong time to give this presentation. We'd just lost Globex because we had overdone the tactics. The company was taking a step back and wondering if it had fired before aiming, yet I seemed to be recommending we just do more stuff, indiscriminately.

While I still believe my critique of Acme's approach was accurate, that the ratio of smart meetings to actual work was pathetic, I couldn't have picked a worse time or a more inappropriate audience for this message. For God's sake, I was sitting across the table from Sterling, a legendary political strategist who hadn't thought about tactics in years.

I concluded my presentation with a quote from Sir Winston Churchill. "However beautiful the strategy, you should occasionally look at the results." Yes, this appeared to be a direct dig at the Globex team, which was basically everyone other than me.

On the other side of the table, Sterling stared at me for a moment. For a man who selected his words carefully, he became quite loquacious. In front of the whole group, he said that he didn't agree with my presentation or how I approached my work. He provided a few examples of how my outpost should view the world, and it made perfect sense. He then launched a broader critique of California, how we got too caught up in minutiae, how we didn't see the forest for the trees, how we needed more ambitious goals and a more daring approach. He was hitting his stride. His logic, delivered in a measured voice that sucked the air out of the room, was incisive and devastating.

"So we have a gap right now between the quality of work we need and the current situation."

When he started winding down, other execs from Red State and New York picked up the slack. They had come here to deliver a message, and they delivered it. Even the timid ones took their turn before settling back into their seats as if they'd just delivered a best man's speech.

"I think we are going to need to get out here more, to make sure you all have the proper support," one of them said.

I met with Sterling immediately after the meeting. He said he'd like me to go out to Minneapolis right away and spend time with one of my peers—a person who was actually succeeding in their job. He said he was going to be coming out to visit me a lot more this year. He wanted to evaluate how I handled my team. He said all of my peers were playing chess while I was playing checkers. I didn't know how to respond to that one. I couldn't think of a more damning statement, considering the scope of my position at Acme. I was being called an idiot in an even voice, without any prejudice—it was just a fact. It was like a girlfriend had sat me down, looked me in the eye and said, "The reason I'm breaking up with you is because you are stupid, ugly, and a bad person."

"Ok," I said.

Later that day, after I'd wandered around outside trying to think of what to do next, Prince Charming called me into his office. "Have a seat, Dan." *Oh, shit, am I going to get reamed a second time?* I wondered. Prince Charming wasn't usually this cordial. He was usually distracted and only half paying attention to those in his presence. "How are you doing?"

"I'm doing ok. That was quite a meeting. How are you doing?"

"I'm fine. I expected that. I'm worried about you. I think you were treated unfairly." This was an interesting sentiment, coming from him. "I'm going to let people know what happened here today. I don't understand why Red State doesn't respect you. You deserve better than this."

Now I understood. My unfair suffering would be his lead message up the chain. I certainly wasn't the only one being criticized in this meeting. I appreciated the support, but I could see what he was doing. By pumping up my suffering and the drama of how I'd been handled, his team's inability to win support for the merger would be brushed aside as the less-interesting storyline.

I was a pawn, but, hey, I'd take it.

I got up the next morning after my meeting and told myself I needed to get my shit together. I went for a long run at five a.m. I swore that I was done with the pills, that I needed to turn things around now or else I'd lose everything. Then I went to work, and the day turned bizarre.

Prince Charming had moved quickly. Sterling, who had already left California, called. "How are you doing today, Dan?"

I didn't know what to say. "Ok. I took a run this morning, and I'm ready to get to work."

"That's good. Hang in there. I'd like to get back out there soon to make sure you have everything you need. Is there anything I can do from here?" His tone suggested he was ready to give me a massage rather than a pink slip.

Prince Charming had pulled off a master stroke. In addition to saving my ass, his message benefited him big-time. It was a Get Out of Jail Free card for the Globex disappointment. It also bought him greater latitude to ignore Red State and the other leadership forces that hewed to their anti-California perspective.

The traveling death squad from our big meeting had their wrists slapped and slinked back to their executive offices licking their wounds. I could tell because the tenor of emails and the comments directed at me on conference calls changed dramatically, literally overnight. They even threw me a few compliments, which was awkward.

I was the person least likely to survive the battle. And just like that, had been spared. It was like I had been playing Pac-Man, and just as I was about to be eaten, I gobbled one of those treats that gave me temporary immunity, and I could run all over the board.

Some odd quirk in this corporate entity had saved me. I'd never figured out how to navigate the company, but at the right moment, I'd somehow stumbled into a safe room. The same arbitrary forces that ruled Acme and had tortured me from the beginning as I tried to achieve the impossible task of pleasing both California and Red State had suddenly saved me.

I felt relieved, of course. But I couldn't get myself to leverage this good fortune with any kind of action plan. I was still cloudy. That afternoon, I met James in the Tenderloin to get my next stash of pills. He was surprisingly coherent and even-tempered. He said he was trying to clean up because he was driving to Sacramento to visit his daughter, and she wouldn't put up with any shit. I was in awe. I couldn't imagine having to do that.

After taking a couple of pills, I walked a few blocks up Nob Hill to see Maureen, who was at a rehab facility at St. Mary's Hospital. She'd been in and out of facilities for months now, trying to recover from her bone marrow transplant. That afternoon, I'd stopped by Chinatown to get her some Shio dumplings she said she'd been craving. For the past few months, she could hardly eat anything at all, and we were all obsessed with feeding her as much as possible. She was skin and bones.

I pulled them out of my bag and placed them on the hospital bed tray in front of her. She seemed to perk up. "Thanks! This is just what I needed." But she didn't touch them.

After our visit, I walked down California Street, heading towards BART. I realized I'd left my sports jacket but when I got back to her room, she was getting some assistance from a nurse. I peeked in and saw her point at the dumplings and say, "Can you please throw those away? The smell is making me sick."

I'd get the coat on my next visit. My feelings weren't hurt. I was just scared because she didn't seem to be getting any better.

CHAPTER TEN

THE END?

After the showdown between me, Prince Charming, and Sterling, I travelled to Phoenix for Acme's Shining Leaders training seminar. All Fourth Levels were required to attend this annual two-night, three-day training. These seminars always had high production value, bright lights, loud music, and lots of interaction. The focus of that year's summit was wellness and featured loud-talking inspirational speakers, each with their own sad backstory. If they hadn't lost a limb, overcome addiction, recovered from delinquency, obesity, or bankruptcy, then someone in their immediate family had.

I settled into my seat at the table with six other people. "Let's talk nutrition!" The speaker, a man with bulging muscles and a shiny head, told us what to eat. Then he told us how much to sleep. We were asked to talk among ourselves and come up with strategies for work/life balance, which was aptly illustrated on the screen by a photo of a lady of indeterminate race walking barefoot on a grassy field. She had extremely healthy teeth, perky breasts, and naughty eyes. I was interested in delving more deeply into her background.

The first person to speak at our table was an older lady who knew it was best to get it over with.

"I like to garden when I come home from work." Yes! That is the right approach, we all agreed.I said I liked to take the kids to the park. And so on.

Then we were provided with devices and asked to fill out a long questionnaire that was intended to anonymously measure our contentment level. The algorithm would then identify specific areas for improvement, starting with the low-hanging fruit. It would encourage us by highlighting aspects of our lives that were particularly healthy. The questions were like these: *When faced with a professional challenge, do you think it is very likely you will persevere, somewhat likely, or not at all likely?* And *In times of crisis, are you the type of person who quickly jumps in to help or someone who is most likely to need help?*

We all worked quietly for ten minutes. *The hell with it,* I thought. I answered honestly.

Then the music started, and our leader told us it was time for us to share our results with each other if we so desired. Each person at my table chose to do so, reading the various machine-driven punch lines spit out by the emotional intelligence algorithm. They all sounded something like this: *You're doing great! Consider eating more leafy greens and other fibrous foods and adding one more thirty-minute cardio session on weekends,* or *Sleep needs to be your priority! Your exercise and nutrition are great, now focus on getting one more hour of zzzs each night :) You deserve the rest!* Mine was along the lines of, *Something is seriously wrong with you. You need to see a mental health professional as soon as possible.*

I chose not to share that. Even the Machines recognized my deteriorating condition. It felt like I had a deep, dark secret to hide, which I did. I was a pathetic loser. But I couldn't imagine giving up the pills and booze. That would be like living without air, love, or joy. Something had to give.

***

My poor sister died on a Tuesday in the Intensive Care Unit at the UCSF Medical Center. That morning, twenty of us gathered in the waiting room. In groups of four, we cycled in to be with her one last time before she left us forever. I wrote the obituary and included this line: *Maureen never saved for retirement—good job, Maur.*

She wouldn't need the money, and she hadn't spent time stockpiling it. She had always opted for life experience over financial security. Maureen had abandoned a successful career in the title business to follow her lifelong dream to start a restaurant, despite having no restaurant experience. If you know anything about the title business, you know it is stable, well paid, and boring. So after years of head-down paper pushing, she said, "Fuck it," and with her partner opened Towles Cafe, a seafood restaurant in downtown Burlingame.

She did what we'd all do if the perfect version of ourselves owned a restaurant. She brought in promising chefs from the city and blues singers from Oakland to perform on Friday and Saturday nights. She hung out with her customers, making friends and sharing laughs and little intimacies. Good customers were often surprised with a comped meal. The ten o'clock no-loud-music ordinance was completely ignored. Her famous cheesy garlic bread was lauded all over town.

A couple of local magicians performed during the weekdays until they became pests. When they were snotty about not getting paid on time, Maureen told them to beat it and locked the front door to applause from her regulars. Life was happening at Towles, and I don't think she regretted any of it as she lay on her deathbed with a small bank account.

At the reception following my sister's funeral, I had four Manhattans and six Vicodins. I also smoked a joint with a friend and downed an Adderall to keep me chugging along. It was a hell of a party, and it went all day. I don't remember it as a sad event. I was flying high, introducing my friends to distant family members, recalling stories about Maureen and generally having a good time. That was the general vibe of her funeral. That's what you get when you celebrate a loved one's life in an Irish family. It was *Finnegan's Wake* minus the resurrection, unfortunately.

On the same night as the funeral, Eileen and I had pre-paid to attend an 80s costume party at a friend's house. It was a fundraiser for our kids' elementary school. Obviously I wouldn't be in any mood to attend, but we agreed that Eileen should drop by. The whole school crew would be there in their edgiest costumes, ready to get seriously fucked up in support of our children's education.

When I got home to an empty house after the funeral—the kids were staying at a friend's—I changed my mind and decided to walk over to the party. I put on my Richard Simmons short shorts and made a beeline for the fun.

Eileen was surprised to see me there. Most people were buzzing pretty hard, but not like me. I poured myself a glass of vodka from the self-service bar and started roaming around. I found a karaoke room—here is where it gets fuzzy—and decided to join a group of moms who were in the middle of a song, really letting loose. It was tight quarters, and I started knocking them around. I kept on singing. Then I remember a big disturbance, and a crowd of people gathered around me. I had fallen over a coffee table and broken two fingers. The physical pain must've opened some doors to other types of anguish. I started crying about Maureen, wailing, actually, in the middle of the party. The entire school community watched in horror. It's hard to imagine a bigger scene.

Some good friends of ours helped Eileen drag me out of there. I could only take a few steps before crashing down on the sidewalk or into the bushes. My arms and legs were bloody. When we got home, Eileen told me to go to bed, but apparently I wanted a nightcap. I poured myself a tumbler full of wine and started upstairs. I fell down, shattering the glass all over the stairs. I kept on going, and when I reached our room decided I needed to go to the bathroom, so I made my way to our dresser.

Eileen had always been borderline OCD, and she'd been more so lately. She liked to keep things neat and tidy. If I used a rag to wipe up kid's pee off the floor, she'd want me to throw it away rather than put it in the washing machine. So you can imagine the horror when I opened her undergarments drawer and unbuttoned my pants. She screamed at me to stop, but I was beyond human intervention. I let it rip, draining a quart of urine onto her socks and panties.

There was a heavy crystal lamp on our nightstand that we received as a wedding gift. As I leaned my head back, eyes half-shut, swaying idiotically, Eileen says she had a strong urge to grab that lamp and brain me. She had the perfect angle, since my back was turned and I was perfectly defenseless. It would have been quite humane. In this *Law and Order* episode, other partygoers would attest that I was extremely drunk that night and had been disturbed for quite some time.

He must have attacked her, they'd agree. I definitely would've voted to acquit.

I would need to quit drinking, or Eileen and the kids were out of there—or, more precisely, I was out of there. The sock drawer incident was the final straw. Eileen now had a mental image burned into her brain that she'd never forget. She only knew about the drinking, not the pills. In my depleted state, I couldn't hold onto that secret any longer. It was eating me alive.

A few nights later, as we lay in bed, I said, "Eileen, I have a secret I need to share." I knew she would assume that I was having an affair. That's the only big secret spouses keep, unless one of them is Walter White. "I'm addicted to Vicodin."

There was relief on her face, more relief than anger, due to my approach (what a bastard). She then got scared. This appeared to be a scene from a shitty Lifetime movie. The one about the husband who washes out of the marriage and only occasionally drops by at midnight, high on angel dust, to see the kids. She jumped into action and said I needed to go to rehab. I agreed.

Without drugs and alcohol, I was faced with having to relearn how to feel normal. My brain had to reestablish its natural biochemistry. Alcohol and opioids had occupied the pleasure centers for so long that their removal created an instant emotional crisis, not to mention a lot of gastrointestinal problems. I would shoulder on because that was the right thing to do for my family, but I couldn't help ask my rehab counselor, "Do people in my situation ever feel happy again?" I was skeptical.

I attended an outpatient rehab every weekday from six to eight p.m for three months. At the outset, I worried rehab was going to be a series of painfully awkward role-playing sessions like the type I was forced to endure at Acme corporate seminars. Instead, it was a thoroughly and almost wholly enjoyable experience. Listening to Joe, the twenty-four-year-old barista talk about how he was trying to calm his inner critic with heroin, or Linda, a seventy-one-year-old upper-crust lady discuss how she drank a bottle of wine before meeting her friends at the farmer's market on Saturday mornings, made me realize that I was among my people.

They all had their own Flip Sides who'd gone rogue, shamed them, ruined their lives. We were banding together, gaining strength to change by hearing about the difficult rebuilds happening in each other's lives. It was so much easier to recognize the mania, the attempts to escape, the foolish and impulsive actions of our fellow addicts and alcoholics, than it was our own. Amid our car crashes, broken marriages, lost fortunes, ruined health, arrests, and other shameful behavior, we all had the same destructive urge to change the way we felt.

CHAPTER ELEVEN

REFURBISHED

Rebounds are lovely things, and that is what I did after sobering up. Changes were made on the Red State team, and I landed a new set of masters who didn't have the same incentives to destroy California. In addition, a number of malcontent legacy members on my own team retired or left the company. Perhaps they left because they hated me. If so, the feeling was mutual, though I was trying to be more spiritual.

I could now bring in my own people, who would be loyal to me and had the right temperaments and skills. Despite my abysmal start at the company, I was trying to convince myself that I could master this corporate system, after all. Maybe the drugs and alcohol had been the cause of my problems.

On the lifestyle front, I was now a member of a twelve-step program, and it gave me the tools to be more emotionally intelligent, when I chose to use them. The advice I received usually involved me turning the other cheek or looking at my own part in whatever work problems I was having. The more I did this, resisting the urge for resentments or illusions of grandeur, the more I could handle the bumps and bruises of corporate life, especially since I had a clean slate, of sorts.

After a year of recovery, I was no longer craving alcohol or drugs. Eileen was happy with my progress. I was grateful for her patience. With the help of Marcie, our recently added marriage counselor, we could both be honest. Eileen let me know how much I had let her down and how terrified she'd been. We were both able to discuss previously off-limit topics relating to our families and also minor grievances, like how she held it over me that I didn't know how to fix the printer. By the end of a year of counseling, we were star pupils, patting ourselves on the back for being able to get through serious problems.

When my body felt better, I joined a gym and started exercising during lunch. I spilled my guts and told my trainer that I had just gotten off pills. He upped the pain quotient of our workouts. I didn't know if this was punishment or a scientific approach to replenishing my dopamine, but it hurt. He was big into ropes and had me try to make waves with these heavy navy-style cords until my arms fell off. Then he'd strap ropes connecting his waist to mine, and I'd pull him all over the gym. It was painful and weird, but I'd do whatever it took.

I was starting to feel outstanding, like a new man, and it showed in my work product.

I had a perfect opportunity to show off my new persona when the entire national public relations team converged on New York for a national planning retreat. From the start of the first meeting, I was on point, cracking a joke here, making a brief comment there. I suddenly seemed to find my footing. I was ready to show them off in the final presentation from our big boss, the CEO direct report who had worked in Congressional leadership and was a big player on the Hill. When he was done with his remarks, he saved half of his time for questions. Everyone knew you needed to be careful with questions. But I was in the zone.

I raised my hand. "We have an issue with a preemption tax in four California cities…" Suddenly, Flip Side appeared around a corner. He jumped in and grabbed my brain. He started squeezing with all his might. "So that's an issue… There are others, but they are California specific…" I sputtered and lost my train of thought while trying to hold eye contact and verbal tone.

People who had only been half paying attention now turned to look. A question that should have been rattled off in five seconds had stalled in mid-air. "I think that what we are facing is a confluence of factors in the public life or in the government, I mean the public political environment in California." What in the actual fuck was I talking about? Something amazing was happening, everyone realized. "So that's where the issue is now in my mind, and I'm not sure, you may need to know this in New York, and I'd like to think there are some other issues like this, before, that we've faced as a company, I mean, at least in California." My face reddened, and I stumbled to a close, holding my expression as best I could.

The big shot looked confused and annoyed. "I guess we will have to look at that, Dan… Anyone else?"

His answer was shorter than my question, which made me look like a jackass. Which I was.

It was a high-stakes blunder on a big stage—a shocking, unforced error at a time when I was trying to forge a new reputation. This man, who didn't know me well, would need to approve and advocate for ANY promotions in the department. Now he likely thought I was an idiot and a wannabe show-off.

When I returned to California, Prince Charming winked and told me, "I heard about your question."

That was when my subconscious started to tell me, once and for all, that I wouldn't be able to make it in corporate America to the degree I needed. Because as 2014 rolled into 2015, I began searching for other ways to make my mark. I wasn't just looking for career stability, I was looking for something significant.

Me searching for something in itself was a potential problem. Why did I need to be always striving for something greater, something BIG? Being a decent man, husband, and father should have been enough. But I craved a big hit. I wasn't willing to give up dreams of an extraordinary life. That was the American Way, as I saw it. But I had to be careful to modulate it and not go off the deep end.

My mind kept circling back to financial independence, a way to get free and clear of corporate America. I didn't have any path to make that happen. Despite that indisputable fact, in my spare time I began listening to financial podcasts and started reading any blogs I could find on early retirement. In particular, the Reddit Financial Independence subreddit was inspiring. It was filled with people who had made enough money to live without income, as long as they budgeted and invested wisely.

Over the years, living in Silicon Valley, I'd spent a lot of time tabulating how much money friends and acquaintances had made on various "exits" like IPOs and acquisitions. Even if they didn't mention the size of their windfall, and most didn't, their houses and Teslas gave them away, as did their vacations to Croatia and Thailand. I always wanted to know the details about their finances.

I remember specifically asking my friend Larry about it on the soccer sidelines. I dug around with open-ended questions like, "Are you able to take some time off?" I couldn't ask exactly how much money he made, so I tried sounding big picture-y instead. "Do you now have the opportunity to work on your own projects?" I felt dirty, but I couldn't help it. I wanted to know.

Of course, he volleyed back the big-pictur-ey vibe. He said, "I've enjoyed startups, and so that's what I'll continue doing."

I'd always been a contributor to my 401(k), as had Eileen. We rolled them over from job to job, consolidating as we went. At the same time that I was building my career, I kept one eye on that little, yet growing, nest egg. I'd search the web and read every article I could about people who'd actually built up enough money to retire at fifty-nine or sixty simply by contributing a reasonable amount on a monthly basis.

The miracle of compound interest is a wonderful thing. The miracle is that you earn interest on your contributions, and then you earn interest on the interest. If we kept feeding our savings, we'd eventually have a lot of money. But to get there, we'd have to commit to steady contributions for many more years.

Even if I'd somehow been able to get the big money at Acme by making it to Fifth Level and then officer, I knew that if I had enough money, I'd leave the company and pursue my own passions, as vaguely defined as they were. I guess I was outside of the zeitgeist of poetic tweets from Silicon Valley billionaires, who insisted it wasn't about the money, it was about the joy of building teams and "making things," their favorite humblebrag.

For most real people I knew in corporate America, some of whom worked at those billionaires' companies, it was about making enough money to get out. The people in the growing financial independence subreddits had an exact dollar amount in mind.

Writing entered my mind as something I was good at, could do in my spare time and might lead to something lucrative eventually. Flip Side couldn't foul me up with anxiety attacks when I was writing, like he could when I was talking.

I discovered Medium, a new blogging platform where unknown writers could be noticed for the quality of their work. In the past, I never had the discipline to follow through with personal writing projects. But now with Medium, I found an audience. That turned out to be the missing incentive.

I began with a shy piece about the leadership lessons I learned running a foot race near my house. A few people read it. Then I wrote about the time my mother vetoed my father's expensive dental treatment when he was terminally ill. That generated a good deal of interest.

As I'm prone to do, I became obsessed. In 2015, I wrote fifty-six pieces, more than sixty thousand words, with 125,000 views. I overdid it. I wrote in the morning, I wrote at night, I wrote on vacation. In fact, Eileen and the kids still joke about how I skipped our last dinner on the last night of one of our family vacations because I was making a final edit to a blog post I was particularly proud of, titled "You Probably Have Low Testosterone."

My pieces became increasingly edgy. They were picked up by *Business Insider*, *Fatherly.com*, *Cuepoint* and a number of other publications. Craig Newmark of Craigslist recommended my story "Silicon Valley Wealth and My Crappy Car." One of Dick Cheney's daughters started following me. Yeah, I was a big deal. Finally, writing and finding an audience scratched my itch for prominence, and it was also a hell of a lot of fun.

While researching one of my blogs, I came across a trove of data about how people are unhappy in corporate America.

I started writing blogs about modern work. My first big hit was "Career Transitions: Crafting Your Medium Humble-Brag"—a sendup of the wealthy, entitled tech bros I envied. I was eating dinner the night after I posted it when I looked at my phone, and I suddenly had more than a hundred new Twitter followers. Medium staff had recommended my piece. Thirty-five thousand people had read it, and, for a time, it was the top story on the platform. I'd hit a nerve.

I started to think of myself as a unique thinker and maybe even a visionary. That is how temporal my self-worth was. I'd gone from the lowest lows to the highest highs in self-regard over the course of a couple of years. That was a good thing, in some respects. Maybe it was the "resiliency" that is the topic *du jour* in psychology circles at the time of this writing. But it isn't exactly the Gary Cooper school of manhood. That would be someone who could slowly, strategically, direct his (or her) own actions toward a goal, never holding themselves in particularly high or low regard. I, on the other hand, gravitated to the poles. Flip Side insisted on glory and usually tripped me up if I was close to achieving it. A man with illusions of grandeur and an inferiority complex, as we say in recovery circles.

After a twelve-step meeting one night, I shared my Medium obsession with my sponsor. I told him about the number of clicks, the glowing comments, the increasing number of followers.

"I think I'm onto something. This could be huge."

He handed me a stale cookie from the table and said, "Take it easy."

I knew what he meant. I ate the cookie, but I was still hungry to do something big to overcome the chip on my shoulder. Flip Side had lied when he promised everything would be ok when I was on drugs and booze. Once clean and sober, I thought I could vanquish him. But he was still screwing up my livelihood. Now he was driving me to write a lot because he wanted the recognition. He was my weakness and also the engine that kept me going. He was like a conjoined twin I couldn't cut out. I needed us to be aligned.

CHAPTER TWELVE

RETIREMENT PORN

I cooled off on Medium, even as my writing ambitions grew. One of my son's friends told him his dad thought I was a show-off. He was right. I was posting a lot of material and encouraging friends to *Share widely!* I also began to think about social media company financials. After Medium secured a big funding round, presumably in preparation for an eventual IPO, a friend sarcastically asked, "How much of that money are you getting?"

He had a point. All of the content I was contributing to Medium made me feel good, but it benefited their bottom line, not mine. Just like with Facebook, YouTube (Google), and the other social media companies, the users were also the products. The platforms owned all of the revenue while everyone else got a pat on the back and social media attention. I kept writing, but I also kept searching. I was looking for something that could give us financial security and ultimately enough money for deliverance, whatever that was.

One day, in late 2015, while searching for a widget article, I came across something about Bitcoin. I remembered that the price of bitcoin had been high a couple of years before. Back then I had thought it was a joke. But now that the price had fallen, a question entered my mind: *What if it goes up again?*

For the next few nights, I read about Bitcoin.

"Bitcoin is dead," the *Weekly Standard*, among many others, announced.

But most stories included quotes from people who still believed in it. They said it wasn't dead.

They said it could never die.

I visited the online crypto communities.

True believers persisted. Some claimed to be economists and investment experts. A popular sentiment was that a single bitcoin, about $400 as I read, would be worth $50,000 in the not-so-distant future. They were certain. Their primary rationale was that only twenty-one million would ever be created. For those keeping score, that's zero inflation for eternity. Once everyone realized it was the best store of value ever invented, the price would skyrocket.

No central banker could change the supply of bitcoin, thereby instantly diluting the value of everyone's stake. If these people from Reddit and other Internet message boards were to be believed, no central entity had any control over Bitcoin. It was decentralized. It was run by thousands of disconnected computers all over the world. I couldn't think of anything else like it.

The philosophy underpinning cryptocurrency wasn't what excited me initially. It was greed, or in polite company, "financial planning." I've always been drawn to the big score, for better or worse. In the same way that I can't help going for broke trying to get a laugh, I can't play it safe at the casino. I have a hard time wagering less than a hundred dollars a hand when I play blackjack. The stories about bitcoin millionaires intrigued me, to say the least. It dawned on me that if you played crypto right, you wouldn't need to worry about compound interest and Father Time.

I gobbled up stories about people who made fortunes buying Bitcoin at a dollar. An investment of $1,500 in 2009 was worth $600,000 in late 2015, despite the steep drop in price in 2014. Whoa. If I'd invested back then, Danny would be enrolled in those expensive guitar lessons.

This was retirement porn, pure and simple, and I became an addict, even though the barrier to actually investing was high. Buying crypto was not something a person in my situation did. Not with three kids, a big mortgage, no nest egg, a shaky career, and an unpredictable flow of income from his wife's business. We'd staked our claim to a moderately comfortable retirement on our 401(k)s experiencing the miracle of compound interest over the next twenty years. Or, more implausibly, my becoming an officer at Acme or landing a C-level executive role at a promising startup. Those were our moonshots.

But it was a hell of a lot of fun to hang out on the r/btctrader subreddit and hear the subversive get-rich-quick kids yak it up. During the day, I attended lobbying meetings with sharply dressed representatives of big finance. They were masters of banking policy who cuddled up to every elected official serving on the committees of jurisdiction over their industry. They wielded a war chest to win friends and influence people. Acme often joined the big banks to lobby for shared policy goals through organizations like the United States Chamber of Commerce. Our companies spoke the same language, nurtured the same dreams. We were going to innovate for consumers like you wouldn't believe, as soon as the regulators removed our consumer-protection shackles.

At night, I began bandying words with a ragtag group of crypto anarchists, Ph.D.'s, Wall Street cast-offs plying their dark arts in crypto trading, and other dreamers, lost souls, snake-oil salesmen, and visionaries who didn't ask anyone's permission to do anything. It felt good. This community was alive. It was electric. They all wanted to upend traditional finance, which they saw as catering to the entrenched 1 percent and deserving blame for the 2008 financial crisis. They intended to get rich doing it.

I decided to go to a cryptocurrency meetup in Palo Alto. As I prowled University Avenue looking for a parking space, I felt like I was on a secret mission. I arrived at the building and walked right in. No one was doling out name tags at the front door.

There were about thirty people in the room, and it looked like the meeting was about to get started. Folks were making their way from the pizza and refreshments table toward the seating area. Good timing, since I didn't know anyone. Bad timing, because there were only two sad pieces of plain cheese pizza left. I poured myself a Sprite and, with my pizza, settled into a seat in the back.

The speaker had a thick German accent, but that wasn't the primary language barrier. His presentation seemed to be entirely composed of numbers. The opening line was something like, "Thank you for coming to the Bitcoin Filigraphic Exponenting Microdanting discussion. Let me start by saying 43%21, but of course, I mean 99946!"

Everyone laughed, because this was apparently a joke about numbers.

What they were discussing was completely beyond my comprehension, allowing me to study the crowd instead. I'd never seen a bigger cast of misfits, freaks, and iconoclasts in my life.

The guy next to me had a long gray beard and army boots. One row over, three Chinese women who all looked thirteen were twirling their pens in tandem. One row in front of me to the right was a sweaty man who didn't blink and asked way too many questions.

When the post-presentation discussion was winding down, I decided to make a quick exit. I couldn't imagine trying to start a conversation with someone in this room. They all seemed enraptured by the presentation. I wasn't about to grab one and say, "I like Bitcoin. Do you?"

As I drove back up 101, toward home, I wasn't feeling deflated, though I hadn't understood anything in the presentation. I was struck by the vibe in the room, the attention this full house of Bitcoin enthusiasts had for the discussion. I'd been to dozens of tech presentations in my life, but I'd never felt that kind of energy, except for maybe a Steve Jobs keynote. But his were more about the Hollywood atmosphere than the underlying technology.

Although the crowd was mainly white males, it was also more diverse than I had thought it would be. There were a lot of older people in attendance. Some were dressed in preppy gear while others were bohemian-looking, borderline homeless in appearance. I'd find out later that crypto early adopters ran the gamut philosophically. Some were Ayn Rand libertarians, and others were hard-left believers in a universal basic income.

I was struck by the differences between crypto culture and the corporate world I was used to. At Acme, I was encouraged to retweet all philanthropy propaganda with a host of research-tested hashtags like #ACMEGIVES, #SOULOFACME and #ACMEASSISTS. Crypto Reddit, Twitter, and message boards were sophomoric, exuberant and completely off the reservation. One woman's email signature was delicious sacrilege to a widget man who'd hosted a dozen safety rallies. It read, *Written while operating a widget.*

The more I learned, the more my mind was blown. *No one knew who Satoshi was? Bitcoin couldn't be shut down by anyone? Billions of dollars were at stake?* This was something out of a far-fetched spy novel that I couldn't put down. But it was all real. I'd seen the people, I'd joined the online gatherings and now, in my spare time, I was soaking it all in at a cellular level, starting to think through what it meant for me.

I started to question what I considered disruptive. The innovations we were talking about at Acme suddenly seemed like boring iterations of existing technology. Pre-IPO companies I'd previously dreamed of joining, like Pinterest, were simply new advertising platforms. Apple announced a new iPhone with a better camera and more glass on the front. Was this supposed to give me a hard-on?

I could relate to the famous quote by early Facebook employee Jeff Hammerbacher. He said, "The best minds of my generation are thinking about how to make people click ads." But now a decentralized digital currency existed without permission from financial institutions or governments. It could be a game-changer for the unbanked. It could create new industries across the world. And, as I would learn, it represented a potential threat to the idea that a centrally-controlled corporation like Acme was the best way to organize economic activity.

***

Back in the real world, things were getting more interesting at work in a bad way. We were working on a new deregulation effort in California. We were having problems, and it was going to be a tough one.

California leadership wasn't happy with my ideas on how we should run the campaign. They pursued a common tactic when faced with a difficult situation. They brought in high-powered consultants. The consultants put together plans, and they were brilliant. Brilliant for them. They were chock-full of recycled tactics, all of which my team would need to actually implement. Outside of meetings with California leadership, the consultants were mainly absent. They liked the bright lights but shied away from the actual work. I couldn't stand the sight of them, but I had to look at them a lot, unfortunately.

With the return of dark times at work, and with no drugs or booze as a distraction, I dove deeper into my research on blockchain.

This is when I learned about Ethereum, a new blockchain with its own cryptocurrency called ether. They said Ethereum was the world computer, with the potential to do to corporations what Bitcoin could do to banks—knock the shit out of them. That caught my attention.

Institutions in the real world seemed to be already grappling with the implications. I came across a blockchain report by the European Parliament that described how momentum could shift toward decentralization at a granular level: "Each time we use a distributed ledger we participate in a shift of power from central authorities to non-hierarchical and peer-to-peer structures."

Wow. As I sat on the curb on Burlingame Avenue one Saturday eating ice cream while the kids finished their piano lessons, I cycled through memories of the various ways I'd screwed up my career. Flip Side had diminished my value by flubbing something in my various workplaces. There was no doubt that I had major flaws, but the corporate environment magnified them.

Could this crazy thing actually make it easier and more enjoyable for people like me with uneven personalities to succeed? Where someone could do the work and make a contribution, but on their own terms, without the need to play the corporate game?

I loved the idea of digital money with Bitcoin, but what Ethereum was promising was altogether more mind-blowing.

Whereas Bitcoin was billed as a new kind of money, ETH was a new kind of fuel. To use the Ethereum blockchain, one needed to pay a small amount of ETH. All of the decentralized applications (dApps) and organizations being dreamed up would require ETH to run, theoretically driving the price up.

By 2016, Bitcoin had existed for seven years and had a sizeable infrastructure behind it. Now ETH was coming up. The price of one ETH was about three dollars when I discovered it, having already risen by 300 percent over the previous six months. The aggregate value of all ETH was about $400 million, significantly less than Bitcoin's $12 billion market cap, based on a single bitcoin price of $380. It seemed to me that ETH could be even more valuable than Bitcoin one day.

But I still didn't own any. Every time I started to think about buying ETH, I had the same feeling I had when I went to Pill Hill. I'd dodged that bullet. Was I really going to do something that might be just as crazy, even though it seemed to make so much sense?

Ever since my addiction period, when I forgot to pay the bills for a few months, Eileen had been in charge of our day-to-day finances. She handled our checkbook, but I managed our family investments and retirement accounts.

While I envied the casual rich in our neighborhood—those financially comfortable through trust funds or stock options—my first priority was to maintain my family's standard of living. Eileen earned a good income as a PR consultant, but my salary, benefits, and annual allotment of restricted Acme stock were what kept us in Burlingame, paid for speech therapy for my daughter, funded summer camps for all three kids and allowed us to keep up with the Joneses, albeit at a lower level. I still drove my beat-up old Volvo. We definitely weren't poor by any stretch, but we certainly weren't in a position to throw money around.

I also recognized that no matter how much I wanted to dream of crypto riches, it was a form of escape. The five twelve-step meetings I attended each week made it easy for me to recognize the similarities between addiction and the mania I was developing. But this felt different. While Flip Side, the addict and escape artist, was super fired up, so was my rational side.

Our nest egg consisted of our 401(k)s and IRAs, which were now worth more than half a million dollars combined. Anything that disrupted our steady retirement contributions would delay our retirement, not to mention threaten our ability to pay for three college educations.

I couldn't stop thinking about how much money we might make if we took the plunge and bought some ETH. At the same time, I couldn't get an image out of my mind of a man standing in front of the infamous Mt. Gox after it was hacked and drained of $50 million in bitcoin in 2013. He was holding a sign that read, *WHERE IS OUR MONEY?* It'd been picked up by the wire services and appeared in newspapers and websites around the world. The guy had a fair complexion, no tattoos, and a forlorn expression. He looked a lot like me. He had obviously lost more than he could afford to lose.

I knew if I bought crypto, I'd be flirting with financial disaster. Neither Eileen nor I had ever been poor, or close to it. We were living relatively high on the hog, and our kids' upbringing was privileged by any definition. Yet we still constantly felt stretched emotionally, financially, and even physically. I couldn't imagine adding poverty to the mix. I couldn't imagine how poor families did it. Not being able to buy your kids birthday presents? Moving from apartment to apartment? There were millions of families like that in the U.S. right then. I didn't want to join them.

And then, in spring 2016, as if a generous upper-middle-class goddess had reached down and blessed us, our financial picture suddenly improved. We received the first windfall of our lives. My mother gave us $50,000 when she sold her home and moved into a retirement community. I'd recently cashed out some restricted stock that had finally vested. And Eileen earned a small lump sum when the startup she had briefly worked for was acquired by Microsoft. Her job was eliminated, but we were able to pocket the money because she picked up consulting clients right away. It was $100,000 total. We'd never had anything outside of our retirement accounts. With my work problems starting up again, this money eased our minds. If I lost my job, we'd be able to survive for some time without having to relocate. We decided we wouldn't touch it.

CHAPTER THIRTEEN

THE EDGE OF A CLIFF

.

Even while I was working long hours on our deregulation campaign, Ethereum was a continual presence on my mind. I found it ironic to be working for a centralized company trying to eliminate centralized regulations by pulling the right levers in a centralized political power structure while I was obsessed with a technology that functioned in the exact opposite manner. The only way to change the rules or manipulate the Ethereum blockchain was through transparent consensus. No oily lobbying or campaign contributions could foul things up for everyone else

The concept of blockchain had made its way into the popular business lexicon. Few knew what it was, and the few who did made a clear distinction between private business blockchains (good) that were centralized in key ways, and the public blockchains (bad) like Bitcoin and Ethereum which weren't controlled by any one person or group. The latter were considered a little dangerous, according to those wise enough to avoid edgy bullshit.

I was happy that the movement was catching on. But the more powerful emotion was fear of missing out.

In the meantime, once again my work status was deteriorating. The consultants were positioning themselves as the company's savior, at my expense. I noticed the big cheeses hedging in their communications on the pieces of the campaign I was working on.

Normally, when something went well in California, they would send something up the chain, which included a thank you to me. Recently, I hadn't been mentioned in those notes. You didn't need to be a Sovietologist to know that if a member of the Politburo was omitted from the group photos, you'd eventually find their body in the dumpster out back. Such was the import of being left off of emails up the chain at Acme. Without constantly feeding the beast, you would eventually grow weak and lose sight of the pack.

***

The great thing about the modern world is that you can quickly become an expert on anything. While walking the dog, I listened to podcasts about Ethereum. When stealing any free time at work, I read about Ethereum. I rejiggered my Twitter feed to follow mostly Ethereum-related contacts. At my usual Friday night Twelve Step meeting, I pulled aside a shaken-looking newcomer. He also happened to be a software engineer. I didn't ask him about his recovery. I asked him whether he'd heard of Ethereum.

At night I played Ethereum-focused YouTube videos on the big screen. My favorites were from DevCon 1, which took place in London in November 2015—the first congregation of the embryonic Ethereum community. The event had a Woodstock feel. By then I knew all about Ethereum's creator, but these videos were the first time I laid eyes on Vitalik Buterin. This was the person who prompted me to write three

Medium blogs, two of which I deleted because they were too fawning, and I'm a grown man. I'm obviously no genius, but I have a curious faith that I can spot one. I believed Vitalik was the real deal.

Vitalik Buterin was born in Russia and grew up in Canada from the age of six. His favorite childhood toy was Excel. He learned about Bitcoin from his computer scientist father when he was seventeen and attending the University of Waterloo in Ontario. He started *Bitcoin Magazine* on the side to explore and write about the cryptocurrency space. Unsatisfied with Bitcoin's limitations, he dropped out of college and took it upon himself to build a new blockchain and an entirely new computer language.

While traveling the world, lodging at various crypto outposts in Zug, Switzerland, the Philippines, and Barcelona, carrying little with him other than his clothes (cat shirts were a favorite), a supply of green tea and a laptop computer, he created Ethereum. Some of the brightest cryptographic minds flocked to Vitalik right away, forming a core of Ethereum co-founders and early disciples. Others, mainly Bitcoin maximalists with a vested interest in Bitcoin's limited blockchain philosophy and the price of its token, didn't like the competition. They called him a Judas to Satoshi's vision, a scammer, a fraud. It wasn't just that these guys were wrong. It was that they were wrong and complete fucking assholes.

Vitalik visited the Bay Area regularly. I learned that he was coming to my neck of the woods soon. That night, I raced down 101, weaving in and out of traffic, determined not to be late to my first Silicon Valley Ethereum meetup. As I entered the Plug and Play incubator office in Sunnyvale, I looked forward to seeing the man in the flesh for the first time.

After a few clumsy words of welcome by an engineer playing host, Vitalik took the stage. It was the exact opposite of how a rock star would enter an arena full of adoring fans. After the organizer's, "We are ready for you, Vitalik," Vitalik walked up in complete silence. He had to plug in his computer so we could all see the screen. For an entire minute, the cord didn't work. More than a hundred of us watched Vitalik and the AV guy mumbling to each other, fiddling with the cord and looking at something on the laptop screen. Finally his deck was up, he turned his head toward us and I could take the full measure of the man.

He had a big head and a skinny body. He was pimply, like many twenty-one-year-olds. He was wearing a cat shirt, sandals, and jeans that looked a size too small. His eyes drew me in. They were intelligent, far reaching, empathetic. I hate the term "old soul," which is normally used to describe the secretly miserable, but Vitalik looked like one.

I'd seen the merciless attacks on him from the Bitcoin crowd, the Twitter abuse and other nasty trolling. He always turned the other cheek. Many of these assaults had a kernel of technical critique wrapped in aggression. Vitalik ignored the vile and calmly, non-aggressively responded to the technical critique. His responses were complete, brilliant and devastating. Call me Homer if you like. I was starting to think this guy could go down in the history books.

The questions directed at Vitalik came from cypherpunks fluent in crypto economics, enthusiasts, experts, and academics. Some were very old, some were very young. Imagine the cantina scene in *Star Wars*. It was a delightfully odd group, without a single big personality pushing business cards.

The first question was something like this: "Vitalik, don't you think that the Byzantine general's dilemma could be exploited by the various geographic nodes in a proof of stake architecture? Is there a way to compile the blockchain that is fault tolerant and aligns incentives with the miners?"

I had no idea what they were talking about. I especially didn't understand Vitalik's response, which he delivered in an even voice seasoned with small bursts of energy, as if he were connected to a gentle electrical current that gave his face a stutter step every so often. I could read people, and it was obvious that his words allowed this guy who asked the question, and others in the room nodding their heads, to understand something that had previously been elusive. There was something right before their eyes that they had failed to see, even though its logic was indisputable, the same way the equivalence of matter and energy was invisible to scientists before Einstein came along and pointed it out. Had crypto's Einstein come along?

One after another, they shot him questions, and each time he identified the heart of the matter and dispensed critical wisdom. I wasn't surprised by Vitalik's performance. I'd recently read an anecdote in *Fortune* detailing similar intellectual wizardry. As part of the profile, the writer followed him into a cryptocurrency boot camp at Cornell. The assistant professor was teeing up a difficult logic puzzle. Vitalik offered a solution before the puzzle was fully described. Of course, he was right.

Vitalik's genius would be critically important for the development of Ethereum, which was completely cutting-edge technology, attempting to do things that were previously considered either impossible or damn near so. He'd be the one shepherding new versions of the blockchain code before it was spun up onto the public net, where it would run independently.

As Vitalik spoke, I thought, *Here it is, a technology in real life, in the early stages, that could take on corporations.*

***

Occasionally, my Ethereum fever broke, and I wondered if I'd gone off the deep end.

Was my growing, almost unacknowledged, desire to invest in Ethereum a desperate attempt by a desperate man to find salvation in whatever came his way? Was this how otherwise sane people were scammed out of their nest eggs, through a combination of a too-good-to-be-true opportunity and undiagnosed mental illness?

Most of my friends in tech, the folks working at Google, Apple, and Uber, were dismissive of blockchain, and none of them had heard of Ethereum. A friend broke out in laughter when I said that I was considering investing in cryptocurrency, as if I'd admitted I was going to buy Smurfberries or Scooby Snacks.

I kept thinking of the developers. In the late 1990s, I saw how Macromedia Flash had caught the attention of the most forward-thinking web designers and developers. More than anything else, that is what made Flash such a big hit. Once the smartest developers became obsessed with the product and started using it in new and unexpected ways, it dominated the web graphics market.

Now Ethereum was pulling in the most talented blockchain developers. They were working on hundreds of dApps.

They were all decentralized. Once these dApps were released into the blockchain, they weren't controlled by a headquarters. They were owned by the users of the dApp. All it took was one to hit paydirt to achieve some semblance of widespread adoption. Use of the Ethereum blockchain would skyrocket, as would the value of the ETH token that powered the network.

I'd been living the problem of work, the problem of gatekeepers, my whole life. So I had no problem imagining the benefits of decentralization through blockchain. It became clear to me that the potential value of blockchain could be bigger than virtually anything else ever invented if it was indeed a new platform for the economy, for the world. The scope of its value was almost unfathomable, like trying to get your head around the number of stars in the sky. I wasn't so naive as to think it would happen overnight. But one of the problems Ethereum was solving was my career. Decentralized work could provide an alternative. So the value of the solution was instantly obvious to me. I speculated that in the years and decades ahead, droves of people—and then everyone—would see its value. Once real dApps were ready to go, and it was hard to know when that day would come, it was a no-brainer. As one of God's creatures and a thoughtful member of the human race, that thought gave me butterflies. As a greedy speculative investor and recovering pill addict, it gave me a rush.

CHAPTER FOURTEEN

PASSAGE

Whenever I read a book or see a movie that covers the first half of the twentieth century, I always wonder what my grandfather, Joe Conway, was doing and thinking at that time. He has always been a mythical, mysterious figure from my family's past. Maybe it's because he died so long before I was born. Or maybe it's because from what little I do know—a handful of biographical facts, a few anecdotes—he was similar to me.

During his youth, the sorrow of departure was the theme of the day in Ireland. Young men and women scraped together money for passage to where they could make a living in distant places, like the United States or Australia. As their ship sailed from the docks, the enormity of their loss was reflected on the faces of their parents, whom they'd likely never see again.

Such was the fate of my grandfather. He left Ireland and arrived in New York in the summer of 1910. He eventually settled in San Francisco, where he met my grandmother and raised a girl and a boy—my father. He owned books of poetry, one of which sits on my nightstand. It is marked up with insights and extemporaneous thoughts. He was a man of letters, like many of the Irish. He received a fine education but had nowhere to use it in his homeland. He had wanted to be a writer, but putting food on the table in America became his focus.

In San Francisco, he found a job in the business office of the San Francisco Water Company, which in those days was a prestigious employer. It was a utility, which provided stability in unstable times. He shepherded his family through the Great Depression with a steady paycheck, reading poetry as release from his day job. He rose through the ranks and became a senior manager.

He defied fate and saved enough to pay for a trip back to Ireland. He planned to depart shortly after his retirement at the age of sixty-five, in 1951. His parents were dead, but he'd see the faces of other family members and friends for the first time in more than thirty years, including his brother James, who had emigrated to Australia and was also coming home.

Reminders of his coming retirement were cropping up in aches and pains as he exited the streetcar one morning, walked down Polk Street and ascended the stairs of his building at 525 Golden Gate Avenue. The stairs took a little longer than usual. The San Francisco chill was a little colder. He'd picked the right time to leave, he thought as he opened his office door, deposited his hat and coat on the rack and sat down in his work chair. He was sharpest in the mornings, but not today. He stood up from his desk to get a drink of water and was hit by the most violent headache he'd ever felt. Then he dropped dead of a stroke.

He'd waited too long to go home.

***

At 10:15 a.m. on May 15, 2016, I exited my office at Acme California Headquarters in San Francisco after wrapping up a brief call with my team. I could feel the folded papers in the pocket of my sports coat. As I walked down Powell Street and hung a left at Sansome, the sun reflected off the buildings, a neighborhood of skyscrapers and street-level brick and glass-fronted startup workspaces. I loved this city, and I loved this time of morning.

I walked into the hushed Wells Fargo lobby with its marble columns and sixty-foot ceiling like Andy Dupree in *The Shawshank Redemption* after he escapes from prison and makes his final play. No one could have known that behind my matter-of-fact body language, I was ready to go for broke.

I told the checker what I was there to do. He ushered me to a desk off to the side where I met George, a bushy-tailed twenty-something who was eager to help. I handed him the papers and the instructions to wire money from my Wells Fargo account to Gemini, the digital currency outfit in New York City that was one of the first established players to offer ether, the currency of the Ethereum blockchain.

"How much will you be sending today, Mr. Conway?"

"One hundred thousand dollars."

I was convinced that Ethereum was the investment of a lifetime, and I couldn't bear to nibble around the edges. Owning a piece of Ethereum would be like owning a piece of the World Wide Web in 1994, before normal people recognized its value. I was no longer normal. I had seen the light, I'd taken the red pill and there was no going back. One hundred thousand dollars was our entire savings and emergency fund.

He paused for a moment and looked at me with a curious look.

"Ok, that shouldn't be a problem. What is Gemini, a bank?"

A man has never been readier to answer a question than I was that morning. I reclined in the bank's chair and explained how this institution would someday be a thing of the past. And if you were smart, George, you'd look into Ethereum and consider buying its token, ether. I wrote it down for him in case he forgot and handed him the folded piece of paper. My modern-day version of "plastics." He thanked me and got back to punching numbers on his keyboard.

As usual after spouting off about Ethereum, I couldn't tell if my subject thought I was crazy or just approaching crazy. George excused himself and walked down the hall. I had a sudden fear that he would return with the manager, and I'd be encouraged to just step outside for a moment, where the guard could ensure I didn't return, while they properly froze my account. Instead he sat back down and said everything was in order, and they were ready to start the wire. The banking machines were cranking up, and the money would leave my account shortly.

My phone vibrated. It was a text from Eileen. I looked at it, and I had the same feeling as when I went to Pill Hill and bought drugs, the same feeling as when I stole a candy bar in third grade. It said, *WTF is THIS?!?!?* It included a screenshot of an alert notifying her that a wire of $100,000 would be leaving our account shortly, headed to something called Gemini.

I had a sudden, brutal flashback to when I told Eileen I was going to start drinking again in the spring of 2007. Our good friends Emma and David were getting married in Napa.

After thinking about it for quite some time, I had said, "I'd like to have some wine at the wedding. It's been a long time, and I know I can handle it. I'm also going to get into great shape."

She had told me that was a VERY BAD IDEA and stormed out of the room. She did not say she'd divorce me and leave with the kids.

A few weeks later, I made my second and final proclamation: "I'm looking forward to having a glass of wine at the wedding."

As I took a glorious gulp of chardonnay on the veranda of that winery so many years ago, I looked at the vines and the beautiful people and thought, *What a wonderful world*. I was delusional. Eileen was devastated.

And now I'd tried to spend all of our money without getting her permission.

I must've paused for a moment too long. When I looked up, George was staring at me.

"Is everything ok, Mr. Conway?"

"Yes, George. I need to check something real quickly. Can you please pause the wire for a moment?"

"Sure." He kept staring at my face, apparently fascinated.

I calmly left the bank. Now Sansome Street was chaotic. A siren bounced off the buildings and into my face. A homeless man screamed at a bird. A group of German tourists wearing dark socks crammed the sidewalk. I called Eileen, and she picked right up.

"Hi! Yes, I've been meaning to tell you about this! I want to put some money into Ethereum, the thing I've been reading about and watching videos about for the last few months."

Eileen had walked by the family room once and found me watching a video of Vitalik speaking on the big screen, when

I'd normally I'd be watching *Homeland* or *Game of Thrones*. That perplexed her. She had stopped in her tracks and stared at the TV and then at me. "Who is that?" she said as she pointed to his face and haunting eyes, frozen in pause.

"It's the inventor of the new technology I am interested in."

This was odd. Since when did I ever watch videos about the inventor of a new technology? She was half-awake, though, and probably thought that if she asked any more questions, I'd talk her ear off about some new obsession. She moved on.

I was careful not to mention that the technology was cryptocurrency, because I knew she could've easily said, "Well, just as long as you don't invest in it," a throwaway comment that would've been problematic.

But now the cat was out of the bag, and there was no salvaging my wire transfer.

"I can't believe you would do this," she said.

"Ok, I'll stop the wire, and we can talk about it tonight."

She was clearly shocked and scared, and rightly so. I'd gone off the deep end before, but at least there were movies, books, and support groups to deal with alcoholism and drug addiction. Was I now a gambling addict? Was I joining a cult? What support was there for families dealing with this type of situation? And hadn't we decided we weren't going to touch our $100,000 security blanket?

I walked back into the bank.

"George, I'm going to need to pause that wire. I need to finalize a few things on my end."

"Sure, no problem, Mr. Conway," he said.

My eyebrows were arched, and I slinked out of the bank and back to my workspace. The rest of that day sucked.

I'd clearly breached the trust of our marriage. I realized how crazy my actions appeared, and I wished I had tried to convince her before making the plunge.

But I fully believed this was a good financial move, a once-in-a-lifetime opportunity. I'd been the best media pitcher at the various PR firms where I'd worked because I did my homework and fully committed to learning the ins and outs of the thing I was pitching. All of the skeptics who wouldn't invest in cryptocurrency reminded me of the PR people who would only do cursory research, then quickly come to the conclusion that what they were pitching was bullshit. They wouldn't get any results. I'd done my homework and believed this was real.

I knew that if I mentioned my desire to go all-in on ETH at my twelve-step meeting, it would be identified as mania, an attempt at escape. Flip Side did want a big score, a short-cut, a reckless attempt to save us, damn the consequences. But I felt in my bones that this was a winning lottery ticket. And I had identified it before most people on the planet.

By March 2016, one ETH was worth $13, a 1,300 percent rise over the previous six months. I was convinced that this was the beginning of an historic climb, like bitcoin in 2013, when one coin skyrocketed from $21 to $1,200 in less than a year. Crypto is crazy like that.

Eileen and I planned to talk after the kids went to bed. With so much hanging in the balance, family dinner that evening was excruciating. I picked over my chicken, rice, and baby carrots. We talked about Annie's extra-credit spelling project in great detail.

After dinner, I straightened up the living room while Eileen took the kids upstairs, read them stories and put them to bed.

At 9:00 p.m., about twelve hours after she received the text alert from Wells Fargo, she walked back downstairs and sat down on the couch next to me.

"What's up?" she asked. This was an unpromising start to the conversation.

"Ok, let me just explain what I'm thinking. The way things are going, we won't be able to retire until we are sixty-five."

My mind always started there when thinking about our finances.

"Ok," she said. "I know that."

I think she suddenly remembered how much she didn't like to talk about finances. She wanted to put the kibosh on the investment, but she'd have to suffer through this first.

"Hey, Ei, just let me go through it, please."

She nodded.

"In the worst-case scenario, we'd lose all $100,000. We might have to start pulling from our equity line if things got dire. But the interest rates are low, and we'd have ten years to repay it."

We'd recently clawed back a Wells Fargo $500,000 line of credit on our home.

"At the end of ten years, we could refinance our house and pay off our line of credit. I'd be working full-time, even if it's not at Acme. Don't forget, we have at least $1 million in equity in our home."

This home equity was always our last safety net, and it was a good one. It'd be hard to tap and might require us to move if we needed the money in the wrong economic climate. But it was there if we needed it.

"In the worse-case scenario, we'd still be able to retire at sixty-five and pay for the kids to go to college. We might have to sell the house when we are seventy and use that money to live as a final safety net, but probably not, if we keep working to sixty-five."

"I don't want to move, Dan. That's not something we should count on."

"I'm not saying that. It's our doomsday plan."

She didn't look convinced. We had both been sitting on the couch. I stood up and pulled up a chair in front of her. I tried to pivot the discussion to the upside.

"Marc Andreessen says that cutting-edge technology always feels cultish and dangerous at first. That's where crypto is right now. That's when you have to invest to make the big bucks, before others are willing to do so."

She didn't look inspired, but at least I had her attention.

"It's perfectly possible that our money could grow by a factor of ten, a 1,000 percent return or more. That's what happened with Bitcoin in 2013. People made a killing! I know it's going to happen with ETH. I can feel it, and I've researched it to death."

Her face softened.

"Bottom line is that losing all $100,000 would hurt, but it wouldn't kill us. But that's not going to happen. The upside is insanely great. If I'm right about Ethereum, if the developers I see at the meetups are right, we'll make a lot of money. We might even be able to retire early! Travel the world with the kids."

She didn't seem angry anymore, but her focus was shifting to the things she still needed to get done before going to bed.

"Ok, listen, I've got to work on an abstract for a client. I can't talk about this anymore. Can you unload the dishwasher?"

"Of course," I said. I opened the door, and a hot blast of steam hit my face. "I'll only do this if you agree."

Then the normal insanity of family life took over, and I feared I'd never be able to buy my ETH.

In the days following our conversation, I tried to be as nice as possible to Eileen in order to improve my chances. I hoped to be more successful than she had been years before, when she tried to convince me to agree to a fourth child. For months, she stayed up past two a.m. doing the laundry, cleaning the house, and finishing her client work. She wanted me to think that everything was running so smoothly around the house, why not add another kid? Instead, she nearly had a nervous breakdown. Late one night, she confided in me that she likely had multiple sclerosis and that she'd be dead soon. As a result, she'd bought Danny a five hundred dollar train set for Christmas even though we didn't have the money, he was three, and I wasn't the type of dad who could assemble it. It turned out she was just sleep deprived.

A week after our discussion about ETH, I was at the gym working with my trainer. I was pulling him all over the place as usual, which still attracted stares. I received a text from Eileen. It said:

Here is the deal. You can invest the money how you choose, IF you agree to the following family trips over the next eighteen months...

Puerto Vallarta
Hawaii (Disney Aulani)
Italy
Disney Cruise
Costa Rica
Plus, the kids and I would like to go to Disneyland every year from now on.

My price is these trips. Take it or leave it.

This chick was crazier than me. Spending all of our money on a speculative investment and taking these expensive trips of a lifetime? Insane. I had a habit of vetoing every extravagant-sounding vacation. But I would've bought a rocket to Mars if it meant I could buy ETH.

Done!!! Thank you, you won't be sorry!

I put the phone down and yelled "YES!" which startled both the corporate types sneaking a lunchtime workout and my trainer, who was still attached to me.

Within two days, our $100,000 was transformed into 6,993 magical ETH at an average price of $14. And Eileen had booked all her trips.

CHAPTER FIFTEEN

GOING ROGUE

At the office, I walked a little slower, I talked a little lower. I was quietly smug for reasons only I was aware of. I'd done something big, something bold.

While everyone yammered on in our Monday morning meeting, I studied each face. Their presentations were more cogent and impressive than mine. But these corporate sharks didn't seem so scary anymore. None of them had the guts to do what I had done.

Howie, the lead consultant, spoke.

"Dan, I think you need to start a green energy communications plan ASAP to counter all of the flack we are receiving from the environmentalists."

Prince Charming nodded. "Yes, Dan, please make that a priority."

Previously, my head would've exploded. We'd been trying to do this for a year, but it had proven impossible. Too many divisions were involved, and none of them was willing to collaborate. Now Howie had teed it up and gotten Prince Charming to assign it to me in front of everyone. Even if the project was possible, it would take at least a hundred hours to get it done. Time we didn't have. Howie wasn't even offering to help. If we pulled it off, he'd get the credit. If we didn't, I'd be blamed.

True, Howie had taken a shot at me. But as a crypto revolutionary, I was starting to feel a little bit like Neo in *The Matrix*. I could see the bullet in slow motion. I recognized the danger, but it didn't concern me. I was starting to feel removed from it all. "Sure, Howie, we'll get right on that."

Trouble emerged on other fronts.

I'd ruffled feathers with the people who created Acme's national philanthropy programs. These particular adversaries were at headquarters, hanging out at the water cooler with the leaders of the company. That was a major advantage employees at every headquarters enjoyed over those at a regional office. They knew it, and didn't hesitate to crush threats to their authority.

I have no evidence, but I suspect that my next hiccup was due to enemies I'd created in Red State. I received a call that someone had made an anonymous complaint to the Acme ethics hotline about a story I'd posted on Medium about an ill-fated drunken alumni cruise during my drinking days. The caller took umbrage that I had tweeted something about an Acme philanthropic effort the day before tweeting this story.

Ok. The alumni cruise story was provocative. Maybe it was a mistake to push that out to my Twitter feed (which, of course, stated *All tweets are my own*). But I found it hard to believe that a random stranger made this connection, found Acme's ethics hotline and called to complain. It felt like an inside job.

I was required to meet with an Acme ethics representative in person. I received a slap on the wrist. I also had to endure a painful call with an Acme executive from Red State. He tried to put my digression in context and told me that he advised his daughter not to post things on the Web, and also his wife, who got quite angry about national politics. Ok. I agreed to be more careful, but comparing what I considered my beautifully nuanced blog pieces to his daughter's sexting and his wife's angry rants about Obama was too much.

I said, "I will try to make them more private, but this is something that is important to me, and I don't think I should be asked to stop writing them."

He said that I should be cognizant of the company's brand, which I represented. I countered that these blogs could be good for the company brand because they were authentic, and we knew from our polling that customers craved authenticity. Maybe an example of someone from Acme writing edgy content would persuade techies and other iconoclasts they could fit in here. Those were the people we kept saying we wanted to hire, right? He said that wasn't the kind of authenticity they were looking for. We agreed to disagree on the most important points. I assured him that I would be more careful.

As we said goodbye, I knew that I was in real trouble. This executive was high up the chain, and he legitimately thought my blogs were vents and/or vile.

One thing you never did at Acme was challenge Red State on social issues, especially if you were from California. You could disagree on policy, approach, and objectives, but the culture of the company came from Red State. Period. Fourth Levels simply didn't write about the things I was writing about. They'd mastered their domains, or at least appeared to, and weren't crying out to the Internet for attention. That wouldn't be good for their brands. It certainly hadn't been good for mine.

But even after this setback, which would have devastated me in the past, I continued to act out.

I had never liked my coworker Bruce Fernen, a suave-looking guy who felt he was hitting his professional stride and couldn't be stopped. I was told by an ally that he had been leaking damaging observations to my boss, which explained why a pool stick had been shoved up my ass that week.

Bruce was always very concerned about his personal brand. He once told me that he felt good about how he was progressing at Acme. To underscore the point, he said, "And my voice is deep." I'd never heard that one before. After that, I noticed that his voice was indeed extremely deep, deeper than mine, which I noticed was quite high.

Bruce was pissing me off, and I'd had it. We were both joining a national conference call from our own offices. Dozens of Third, Fourth, and Fifth Levels from around the country would be joining this particular call. Right when the call opened up, before he could announce himself, I did it for him in falsetto, an octave higher than Michael Jackson. "This is Bruce Fernen. I'm looking forward to this call. Thank you."

Pause.

"Thanks, Bruce," the stupefied host from Oklahoma responded.

To the professionals out there: feel free to use this technique to make friends at work!

The Bruce Fernens of the world could take it, I thought. They didn't seem to have much of a Flip Side. Or they were better at hiding him. They seemed to have confidence, that attribute that always eluded me. It pissed me off that the corporate culture and dynamics of this beast rewarded the Bruce Fernans of the world. I was certain he'd pass me in the pecking order. I couldn't help but take a shot at him.

And now, with crypto running through my veins, I had my own form of confidence, in the shape of an escape hatch.

CHAPTER SIXTEEN

THE DECENTRALIZED AUTONOMOUS ORGANIZATION (DAO)

n 1962, my parents paid $6,500 for our cabin at the Russian River. They scratched and clawed to come up with the down payment. My dad picked up a night job at Sears at the same time he was working full-time as a seventh-grade teacher and earning a master's degree in education. My mom held to a tight household budget to make ends meet. Getting a summer place, no matter the condition, was her goal. She hated the year-round fog of Daly City, even though it was close to my dad's job.

The river house was our family temple. That was where the Conway vibe was the strongest. My brother and cousin, both musicians, played Bob Dylan and Tom Petty songs late into the night as we all sang along. One year, a small fire started in the living area, which Maureen turned into a water fight with fire extinguishers once the fire was out. My brother even wrote a family song about the river which started with the lyric, "All I ever seem to do is work all the time."

On Memorial Day 2016, all of the remaining original members of my family were there: me, my older brother Joey, my sister Kathleen, and my mom, who was still going strong at eighty-six. We'd always been fairly close and willing to share what was going on in our lives. Since there was no

TV at the cabin and limited cell reception, it was the family venue most suited for conversation. Considering my current struggles at Acme, this would be a perfect opportunity to unburden myself and get some moral support.

I started talking, and I wouldn't shut up. But all I could talk about was ETH.

"Listen, I have something big to tell you. I've discovered a new digital currency, like bitcoin. It has a cult following in the tech scene, and I think the price is going to explode upwards. This guy Vitalik Buterin who invented it is a genius. He's only twenty-one, and he was born in Russia. He learned Mandarin in his spare time!"

And so on.

We have a family friend who—before being institutionalized—started using colors to describe the days. "Today is a red day. That means tomorrow should be orange," he'd say. Kathleen told me later that when I explained how blockchains are based on solving little puzzles —miners competing to process blocks—she thought I might be developing schizophrenia. But as a former addict and penny stock speculator herself, she leaned in to hear everything, anyway. "What are the chances it doubles, Daniel?" she asked.

I was impressed with her immediate focus on the upside.

"It could go to zero, but I don't think that is going to happen. Doubling is nothing. If it works, it could go up a 1,000 percent, like Bitcoin."

After doing her own extensive research, she bought a big stack of ETH a few months later with money from a home refinance and the remainder of her 401(k).

My brother Joey said he could tell I was on to something. He knew I was prone to passions, but he'd never seen me like this. He said he wanted to buy some ETH, but he wasn't in any rush. He eventually bought a big chunk.

"How much have you put in?" he asked.

"I've made a pretty big investment."

Normally we talked freely about money. It wasn't a taboo subject in my family, like it was in Eileen's.

"Wow, if you aren't going to spill the beans, it must be a lot!"

It was getting late, and my mother stood up and headed toward the back bedrooms. "Boy, it sure sounds good, Daniel, but I really hope you haven't bet too much." She stopped on the way to wipe the dust off a table of knick knacks. She straightens things up when she's nervous.

Unfortunately, something was happening right then on the Ethereum blockchain that would concern everyone who owned ETH. On April 15, the Decentralized Autonomous Organization (DAO) had launched as the first ambitious Ethereum-based decentralized application on the Ethereum blockchain. The DAO was the embodiment of my two great hopes: that a decentralized alternative to the corporation was possible and that successful projects would cause the value of ETH to rise exponentially.

The problem was that the DAO was years, maybe decades, too early. Ethereum was still experimental technology. By comparison, the DAO was nearly science fiction. It aimed to run an entire corporation with governance, long-term planning, and day-to-day administration on the blockchain immediately. Blockchain technology was still so new. It was like trying to create YouTube in 1995 before LTE, when most people were just learning about email. The tech simply wasn't there yet.

It seemed to me that the project was being rushed out before its time to ride the wave of interest in Ethereum. I listened to a dozen hours of podcasts featuring the leaders of the DAO. I didn't think they were ready for prime time. There were a lot of questions. Their answers were basically, "I don't know. We'll see."

The DAO's launch generated massive coverage, including articles in *The Wall Street Journal* ("Chiefless Company Rakes in More Than $100M"), *Bloomberg* ("Blockchain Company Wants to Reinvent Companies") and the *New York Times* ("A Venture Fund with Plenty of Virtual Capital, But no Capitalist.")

On June 18, 2016, my forty-fifth birthday, Eileen, the kids, and I walked to our favorite breakfast spot. I glanced at my phone and noticed crypto Twitter was blowing up. The DAO had been hacked, and everyone was freaking out. This was not a flaw in Ethereum, but it hardly mattered. The DAO had stolen the headlines for the past month. Now it had failed spectacularly, and everyone was running for cover.

The price of ETH dropped 40 percent over the next three days. There was no telling when the bleeding would stop.

At this stage of its development, cryptocurrency in general and Ethereum in particular were prone to extremes. Mind-blowing highs and earth-rattling lows. ETH is a currency of black swans. If it works, it may black swan much of corporate America, but in the meantime, many black swans could destroy it, including hacks, bugs, regulations, cartels, and competitors. This thing I'd fallen in love with was so revolutionary, so cutting edge, so rife for attack, so disruptive and so exotic, that it could explode into nothing at any time or rapidly ascend as the ownerless foundation of a new decentralized economy, as zealots like me thought it would. For an addict, a dude who was mad as hell, an adrenaline junkie with illusions of grandeur, for the drunken Irishman trying to express himself even when he was sober, ETH's insane volatility and high stakes suited me perfectly.

So when the DAO was hacked, I wasn't worried about losing my investment. I wanted to get more ETH. It was poised to go lower in the short term. The handwriting was on the wall.

I could sell all of my coins and buy back lower to increase my already-large stake.

On June 19, as Eileen watched TV downstairs, I logged into my Gemini account from our bedroom and started selling big blocks of ETH. The order books were thin with limited liquidity in those days. It wasn't long before people on r/EthTrader commented that something big was happening. "Holy shit, someone is selling massive chunks of ETH on Gemini" was the gist of the scared post from a trader fearing a crash. The price started dropping, reducing my ability to get a fair price, as other traders tried to get out ahead of the broader dump I was inadvertently creating.

Most of the people on the boards, at least those who were commenting, had bought ETH during the initial crowdsale in 2015. Anecdotally—there is no way to know for sure—most had invested less than a thousand dollars (denominated in bitcoin) and owned between three hundred and three thousand ETH. I had much more to gain and much more to lose than most. I wasn't the biggest whale on the boards. A whale was someone with a huge stack of coins. But after reading lots of posts over many months, I knew I was in the upper echelons. As I finished offloading all of my tokens, someone commented, "Looks like the Winklevoss twins are selling." But it was only me.

My plan was to watch the price drop for the next few days, then pick up all my coins at a thirty percent discount, allowing me to increase my stack. Except it never works that way.

After a long day at work on June 22, I decided to take the kids to the local pool for a swim. I drove there but didn't see much of the road, because virtually the entire ride I was staring at my phone, watching the price of ETH *go up*. I was terrified. I might miss the launch of the rocket ship, which could happen at any time, despite the DAO fiasco. I could hardly stand myself, not to mention care for the three darlings in the back seat whom I'd loved just an hour ago. But I couldn't exactly turn around, drive home and tell Eileen I needed to make some crypto trades while the kids dissolved into pouts and tantrums. In fact, I hadn't mentioned the DAO disaster to her at all. After we made our initial investment, she never asked about Ethereum, and I wasn't about to use this opportunity to tell her, "You wouldn't believe what's happened!"

We were going swimming, dammit, even though ETH was rising quickly, and there was nothing I could do about it until they were in the pool. So I started slathering suntan lotion on them. I'm obsessive about this because my aunt died young of melanoma. They were going to get their standard full-body lotion application, just at a faster rate and with more force. A dad in the lounge chair next to us stared at me, because I was obviously a very serious asshole.

Finally, they were in the pool, and I could log into Gemini from my phone. I was going to get back in, no matter what.

I've found crypto trading akin to playing blackjack in Vegas. Meaning, you're going to lose. If you have nineteen, the dealer's about to get a seven of clubs to make twenty-one. If you have twelve, your hit card is going to be a joker. So as I desperately signed in and started buying big blocks of ETH, the price kept shooting up. The bots and gods and other traders all somehow knew that I was desperate, so the price continued to rise.

Since exchange trades are public and viewable, albeit anonymous, every trader could see that a whale was buying back in. The scramble was on to buy their coins at a lower price before I scooped everything up for myself. That's what I did. I basically bought up all of the coins that were available at that time on Gemini. This set off a bidding war. My final trade, after which I finally looked up to ensure my kids hadn't drowned, was a market buy, a desperate, determined play to get my coins no matter what. A market buy is when you buy whatever coins are available at whatever price, even if the price is wildly high.

Over the course of an hour, I bought back all I could, 5,584 ETH at an average price of $14.40. I'd lost 20 percent of our stack, a heartbreaking amount. I wanted to cry. I vowed to never, ever try to time the market again with a short-term trade—and I never did.

Then the ETH price started dropping, just as I predicted it would, just not on my timeline. By early July, ETH had fallen to $10.12. Our investment was $45,000 in the red. Fuck.

I thought of solar panels. My parents got caught up in a late 1970s solar energy tax shelter scam. After hearing about the opportunity from their accountant, they attended a slick day-long presentation. There were scientists in white lab coats and smoke billowing from smokestacks. Many doctors and lawyers had invested, my dad later explained.

My parents put in ten thousand dollars, a lot of money for them, and in return they owned shares of solar panels located somewhere in the desert. Soon after, they stopped hearing good news from the custodians. Then they stopped hearing from them at all. Like the doctors and lawyers who also got suckered, they lost everything.

They were sure about those solar panels like I was sure about Ethereum, although I don't think they had solar panel hats, t-shirts, and phone cases. I knew Ethereum wasn't a scam. But was I destined for the same fate as those hapless professionals from the 1970s who bought an investment based on a sound idea that would never pay off?

But I processed these thoughts at an *intellectual level*. I still had the strongest *feeling* that ETH was going to go up, despite my rational brain telling me that these things didn't usually work out. The mountain I'd had to climb before investing was too high for me to consider climbing back down. Flip Side helped me get up, but he certainly wasn't going to help me down. He'd cut the ropes, in fact. We were going to make it big and set the record straight, once and for all. There was no going back.

CHAPTER SEVENTEEN

DELETED

I knew my fate at Acme was sealed when I checked my email one night a few weeks after our dereg campaign went down in flames. New York sent me a note informing me that the consultants were staying on board, even though the campaign they had been hired to work on was over. When I asked why, they responded, "Prince Charming wants them to stay." No one had even bothered to tell me. I suspected they would never need another substantive response from me.

I breezed through the next few days. Then on Friday afternoon, I received an email from Kermit, yet another big shot from New York. *Hey, Dan, I'm going to be in your neck of the woods on Monday. Can you meet me at your office at ten a.m.?*

This was it, I told Eileen. They were coming for me. These were the possible outcomes, as I saw them, in order of likelihood:

1. I'd be put into another position. This happens all the time. A make-believe "special project" would be created, which would give me about six months to find another position before that job was eliminated.

2. I'd be put on probation. Before firing me, they would need to document the hell out of it, and this meeting was the first step.
3. I'd be fired. They'd explain my severance package, which I hoped would be generous for someone at my level with six years at the company.

I always wondered why people who were about to be executed in grim documentaries would simply follow orders. Why would they dig their own graves while their killers stood ready to pull the trigger once they were done? Why didn't they turn around and smash the guy in the face with the shovel? Why not make a last-ditch effort to escape? At the very least, they'd hurt the asshole who was about to put a bullet in their head. As I greeted Kermit and was introduced to Fuckface from HR who would be joining us, I figured it out. They were tired. They wanted it to end. They knew their fate, and making a big fuss wasn't going to change anything.

Kermit and Fuckface asked if I could please find a conference room. Was it cruel and unusual punishment that I couldn't find a room? It certainly was macabre. Our goddamn open-office environment meant that all of the conference rooms were filled with people trying to escape the fishbowl. It was hard finding a proper location for a corporate execution, but I was trying my damndest. I finally found a great spot, tucked into the corner of a section of the office that was under construction. Very little foot traffic. Soundproof. Perfect.

Kermit was very short, with a nice head of hair. Fuckface was tall, gaunt and unsmiling, with thick makeup.

"Well, Dan," Kermit began, "you are not in our plans for the future. Fuckface and I want to give you an option that will help you make your transition away from the company. We've discussed your situation with one of the public relations firms that is close to the company. They would like to contract with you as an independent consultant. You have talents that you can put to use for them. If you agree to do so and resign from Acme right now, we can make that introduction. We hope you choose this option. If you do, you can stay for two more weeks, leave the company on your own terms and enjoy one more month of healthcare coverage. If not, today will be your last day, and we will escort you out of the building after this meeting."

"We will also take your iphone and your computer, which are company property," Fuckface added. As if I were going to secretly slip my iphone down my pants. She wanted to make sure I recognized their leverage. Losing my job and my iphone on the same day, without having a chance to download my contacts and other stuff, would add insult to injury. I suddenly regretted not getting a second device for personal business.

If I took this offer, I'd be leaving my stock options on the table. No severance. We'd lose our healthcare at the end of the month and have to buy it on the open market. And the arrangement would be a handshake deal, no written contract.

I'd always wondered what happened to those desperate forty and fifty-somethings who applied for lower-level jobs on my team. This is what had happened to them.

But could I really complain? I'd sabotaged myself, even if my fate had been sealed anyway.

I kept my cool and never got emotional. I'm a pussy during normal business interactions, but I get steely calm when I'm truly in a jam, like Michael Corleone lighting that guy's cigarette. Or so I like to think. But there was no doubt about it, I was wounded. Contemplating getting fired had a much different impact on my psyche than actually being fired. I was seriously being FIRED. I kept turning it over in my head.

It seemed to me that the purpose of their approach was to squeeze me. Since I hadn't had a written plan documenting a subpar performance, I might have an opening to sue the company. If I officially resigned that day, I'd nullify any legal case. But that didn't bother me. They were firing me because they thought I was an idiot, and they also needed a scapegoat for our big defeat in Sacramento, not because of my advanced age, whitish skin color, or raging-hot heterosexual orientation.

I asked if I could take an hour to call my wife and think it over.

"Why would you need to do that?" Fuckface asked, staring deeply into my eyes. "This is a more generous offer than you should expect." Apparently this woman whom I'd never met before, who flew here from god knows what state, had a very firm opinion of my worth and what I should expect after six years with the company. She was the embodiment of the Acme Machines... cold blooded and malevolent. And I was simply a digit that needed to be deleted from the code like the bodies flushed out of the Matrix once their energy was harvested.

"Because this is a very big deal, and I need to gather myself for a moment," I said. "Don't you think that's a reasonable request?"

To my utter fucking dismay, she actually started to smirk, like I was her adversary to be defeated rather than a middle age man being fired from his job. "This is a very generous offer. I don't think we can..."

I was about to crawl down this demon's throat when Kermit interceded. His look reminded her that they were there to kill, not torture. After six years at the company, taking a short break to think it over, even if the choice seemed obvious, was entirely reasonable. Fuckface's display of insensitivity was no surprise. Nearly every HR person I've dealt with is sadistic.

My signature or my brains were required on that resignation note, and so I signed it. They left the building, and I went about my morning as if nothing had happened.

***

On my last day, when it was time for me to leave the building, I said a few goodbyes and headed for the elevator. The doors shut as I watched a group of now-former colleagues in the conference room hammering out the details of an event I'd been involved with just a few days before. I had thought that a few of my most loyal employees might walk me out. I didn't want them to quit, I just wanted them to exit with me, like someone walking by my side to the gallows. They didn't, because they had jobs to do.

I saw a friend later that afternoon in our neighborhood when I was taking the dog out. He walked with me for half an hour while I told him exactly what happened, blow by blow, not hiding the fact that I'd been spit out. That was the way I'd always processed things, by getting it out of my system. That night at a Cub Scout event, while the kids bobbed for apples, I told a few other friends. It was like I was telling everyone, "I just died!" Talking it out, sparing no humiliating detail, helped me drain the poison.

I'd heard divorced people who'd struggled in their relationship for years say they were happy once they got divorced. In this instance, Acme had taken the initiative and dumped me.

Like a newly divorced person, I was in shock. But I also knew I was out of a situation that made me miserable.

Eileen was very supportive. It had been clear to her long before that I was being squeezed out. She was proud that I'd gritted it out until the very end. So she wasn't upset with me. We both knew I couldn't afford to sit around, though. I needed to start up a new career and make some money.

It was time to see if blockchain and cryptocurrency were make-believe or the real deal.

CHAPTER EIGHTEEN

ZEALOT

E ileen and I decided to start our own PR firm. She was already a successful consultant. We'd combine forces and go after bigger clients. I'd focus on crypto/block-chain. My hunch was that few PR consultants understood this world. I knew that the demand for strong communicators in the space was growing. There was a gap between the hundreds of fascinating projects brewing and conventional wisdom, which suggested that the whole industry was fraudulent. This discouraged professionals from joining in. We launched Zealot Communications on October 1, 2016.

Setting up my own systems was therapy. I bought a Google Chromebook, procured my own personally paid-for iPhone, and put up a website with SquareSpace. I updated my LinkedIn profile, changed my Twitter page, revised Medium, and posted my new career status on Facebook. While I was free from Acme, I was still in the grips of the centralized behemoths that controlled the modern Internet. These massive gated communities have taken a cut of everything, sold our data, and made all of the rules.

It wasn't supposed to be this way. In the 1970s and 1980s, Tim Berners-Lee, the inventor of the World Wide Web, was driven by the idea that the Internet wouldn't be owned by anyone, that it would be a free and rollicking information superhighway. He is now working on new blockchain-heavy standards for what is collectively called Web 3.0. The goal is to move the Internet away from the current power brokers and give freedom and control back to the people. He is hopeful, even though the challenge is steep. In a *Wired* article, he said, "You can make the walled garden very sweet. But the jungle outside is always more appealing in the long term."

Someday I hoped blockchain would disrupt their stranglehold with decentralized alternatives, but that day had not yet come.

I pounded the keyboard and put out a blog post. It encapsulated my revenge-first perspective that dovetailed with my belief in crypto. I used the upcoming Ethereum developers conference as the hook:

Personal Computing Devices and the Coming War

All the real action in computing has been out of our grasp for quite some time. Yes, that supercomputer in your pocket is better, faster, stronger than last year. But the thrust of its development has been to better acclimate it to the great nipple of computing power in the sky: The Cloud.

The Cloud, i.e. server farms, are where the real action is. These vast racks of processors in air conditioned rooms, under armed guard, run our apps, set the rules, process our transactions, and upgrade the operating systems of our slave clients. Unplugged from the cloud, your computer is nothing.

Blockchain is a buzzword that describes a rebellion in District 12. Blockchain apps run on decentralized networks—served and maintained by the computing devices of hundreds of thousands of people around the world. None of these people control the network. Each of them is rewarded individually with cryptocurrency for contributing their computing power towards its maintenance.

Bitcoin is the oldest blockchain, and it is already three hundred thousand times more powerful than the world's fastest supercomputer, at least 100 times more powerful than all of Google's server farms combined.

The bounty of decentralized networks is the wide distribution of the spoils of innovation. On the Facebook-like dApp (decentralized app) of the future, users will be rewarded if they grant access to their personal shopping habits; on the AirBnB-like dApp of the future, the server farms won't be able to increase their cut, and a true peer-to-peer marketplace will flourish.

A reckoning is coming, which is why you are starting to hear about blockchain in nervous corridors of power, among the disenfranchised and among the awake. Rebellions can be messy—the Bitcoin blockchain has been supplanted by Ethereum as the most decentralized network, the one less likely to ever be controlled by server farms. But all block-chains are a step in the right direction.

Next week, at the Ethereum Devcon2 in Shanghai, thousands of developers from every corner of the world will gather. More than one hundred dApps will be showcased, discussed, and considered. Will one of these be the killer dApp that sets this rebellion in motion?

I'd previously written a Medium story in May 2016 about how I had come to the decision to make a large investment in ether. It was a hit and had been read by fifteen thousand people. I created an online publication called *Citizen Crypto* with the goal of building on that audience and establishing my reputation in the community. I wrote about how blockchain could prevent fraud and embezzlement ("Organized Crime Hates Ethereum"), cut the bullshit and bring back integrity ("Your Sourpuss Grandpa Will Love Blockchain"), simplify and verify medical records ("Presidential Health on the Blockchain"), and prevent data breaches ("Yahoo's Data Breach and the $12B Antidote"). I also wrote a piece with recommendations for PR professionals working in crypto ("Mainstream PR, Meet Cryptocurrency") as if I were a grizzled veteran rather than someone figuring out if I could make a living in the space.

Through one of Eileen's contacts at the venture capital firm Redpoint, I won my first crypto account, a well-known and respected early cryptocurrency wallet company called BitGo. Their CEO, Mike Belshe, was a sharp pioneer in the space. I impressed him with my knowledge of the cryptocurrency universe, which by that time was extensive, up to a certain technical point. He brought me aboard to work on an upcoming launch. Eileen and I were relieved. We had no idea if projects and companies in this space would pay for PR until they did.

I accelerated my outreach to the crypto community, and it felt great. I wasn't going to turn anything down, no matter how small. I figured the best way to find clients was to start a meetup group. I called it Ethereum Economy—SF Bay Area. I wrote a Medium blog ("Enter the Ethereum Economy") that breathlessly explained my charge:

For those of us who believe in decentralization and have committed to the cause as a funder of a particular token, as a career move, or as an evangelist—this is a gathering place to figure out how we can help, compare notes, talk strategy, hear interesting speakers and network. We are going to need to pull on one another as this thing heats up and the real ride begins.

Two hundred people signed up. My first meeting featured a presentation by Martin Koppelman of the prediction market dApp Gnosis, one of the hottest projects at the time. Six months later, it would be valued at an eye-popping one billion after its Initial Coin Offering. I invited my sister Kathleen and a couple of friends who were tech-savvy, mildly interested, and willing to do me a solid.

Martin's presentation was thorough. But it was so unbelievably dry and inscrutable that I wanted to cry. After an hour of him reviewing numbers-heavy slides in a small font with generous tangents featuring a soup of concept words like "random beacons," "plasma diospheres," and "the skyline number theory," he mercifully concluded. One of my friends shot me a look that said, "You've harmed me, and I won't forget this." The other one just stared straight ahead, appearing to be in a trance. Most of the crowd seemed to love this stuff, though.

My vision for the meetup was that I'd attract normies like me, maybe a few lawyers, some tax guys, and soft-boiled tech early adopters. We'd all speak English, for once. But this stuff was early, and the only ones willing to show up were professional mathletes, with just a smattering of dreamers like me who grasped the concept at a deep and emotional level but didn't understand how it worked at a granular tech level. Regardless, I was psyched to have started something that brought these top-tier minds into the room. I was on my way.

The only thing that wasn't making sense was the price of ETH. The fundamentals of Ethereum couldn't be better. Transactions were rising daily, hundreds of dApps were now in development, the hashpower (processing power) of the Ethereum blockchain had grown by leaps and bounds over the previous three months and the developers conference had sold out in just a few days. The DAO disaster had happened six months prior, which is a lifetime in crypto, where everything moves at warp speed, because every player is animated by money.

While the Ethereum platform was gaining strength, the price of ETH continued its slow-motion drop. This began after the DAO hack when a splinter group formed a copycat coin. By November 28, ETH had fallen to $8.81, putting us down 50 percent. We'd only realize that loss if we sold. We had no plans to do so, but we didn't have an unlimited runway. I constantly lurked in r/EthTrader, which was populated by crypto investors, speculators, true believers, and also trolls spreading doubt and hoping to cause a panic for the fun of it or so they could buy cheap coins. Many posts like these confidently predicted the price of ETH was going to drop even more and might not ever rise again:

Ethereum has no utility or even realistic impending utility at the moment. The bubble has popped until a use beyond academic masturbation is discovered. And when that use case is discovered, I might invest. Not sure it will be represented by ETH necessarily.

Eth isn't used for payments and there are zero dApps that are widely used or even useful at this current time. It's already obvious from the price action today there aren't any buyers for Eth right now.

ETH dumping hard. Last chance to exit. I am confident we will see $3-6 before year's end.

Crap. I used to punch numbers into the calculator on my phone to figure out how many ETH we'd be able to buy at a particular price and how much we might make if ETH rose to certain dollar amounts. Now I'd punch numbers to figure out how much of the $100,000 we'd lost. It was more than $60,000 at this point. That was more than we'd ever had in savings, nearly half the once-in-a-lifetime nest egg we'd received the year before. At a time when I didn't have a full-time job.

Nighttime was my witching hour. I couldn't sit through an entire movie or family dinner without feeling antsy and distracted. I wanted to go off somewhere by myself and work the numbers, see if I could find a different, more reassuring way to analyze our financial picture. I started going to bed earlier. I also tried my best to stay off Reddit, where every night, trolls invented new ways to tell us we were doomed.

Eileen was oblivious to all of this. She was taking the ignorance-is-bliss route. If I'd never mentioned the crypto investment again, there was a chance it would never come up.

At least our move to start Zealot Communications was going well. We were featured on the *Mr. Reubot* podcast. *ETHNews* wrote a story about us. At BitGo, I was exchanging emails with heavy hitters and crypto legends like Erik Voorhees, who invented the first popular Bitcoin application, Satoshi Dice, and was now running ShapeShift, a service that allowed one cryptocurrency to be easily exchanged for another. At meetups, I met other blockchain luminaries, including Andreas Antonopoulos, the well-known cryptocurrency evangelist who'd written the definitive book on Bitcoin and was now working on one for Ethereum. I interfaced with the executives at the powerful and mysterious OKCoin, a Chinese-based BitGo client and the largest digital exchange in the world by volume.

At the BitGo holiday party, things were coming together nicely. Eileen and I sat at a five-star restaurant at the base of the Bay Bridge with a million-dollar view. I met one of their loud-talking VCs, chatted with a wasted administrative assistant, and spent time with a guy in Singapore who had been ported via video to a robot that rolled around the restaurant, running over people's feet.

Mike complimented my contributions to the company in front of everyone. I was having a blast. I believed in this technology and the changes it would bring to society. I was legitimately interested in each bit of content I read, and I tried to make sense of everything and put it in context.

Unfortunately, ETH kept dropping. By December 28, it hit $7.12. Our original $100,000 investment was now worth less than $40,000.

It looked like we'd bought at the top. We were in for the long term, sort of. We could handle a decrease in price, but if ETH stayed depressed or fell further, the strain of holding it would become a crushing weight on our shoulders, at the same time that I was forging a new career.

But my confidence in Ethereum and its ongoing development was as strong as ever. I couldn't avoid the dangerous thought that ETH was a bargain at these prices. I couldn't will the price to go up, but I could reduce our average cost per ETH by buying more. Once I spun that idea in my head, I couldn't let it go. If one hit of acid wasn't working yet, might as well take another.

As I walked to pick my kids up from school, I punched numbers to figure out how much our average cost would be reduced if I bought different amounts at these low prices. The more I bought, the bigger my stack, and the lower my average cost would be. These numbers were a lot more fun than the ones I'd been staring at for the past three months.

But we didn't have the money. We'd already invested an outrageous sum and our entire nest egg. The only pool of funds available was credit—the line of credit on our home. Racking up a big debt on our home equity line would put us in movie territory. The movie where the man ends up divorced and living on frozen dinners. His uneducated adult children use words like "ain't" and phrases like, "No one ever done that before, me don't think."

Eileen's strategy to deal with ETH volatility was to tune it out completely. She didn't want to talk about it. Now that her trips were scheduled, she told me I should do what I thought was right. She was happy that I had a PR client in the crypto space and was making money. The BitGo holiday dinner, attended by legit VCs and the normal tech types she was familiar with, gave her confidence that crypto wasn't just me and a group of folks from the mental hospital.

I set up a call with a couple of other Ethereum enthusiasts I'd met along the way. I told them that I was thinking about making another investment. Each said they wanted to buy more, but they didn't have the cash. I said I was considering putting $15,000 more in, much less than I was. They laughed and said that was a bigger play than they could make. I was reminded that I was already in deep. I was a whale, and I'd bet more of my net worth than anyone I'd ever heard of.

Had my measured risk morphed into self-destructive recklessness? Was I getting too emotional about this investment? I thought of my two great-grandfathers. One shot a man in the 1860s in a bar fight, and the other had been shot and killed in a bar fight around the same time. Both apparently lost their cool and acted on a dangerous impulse. And it cost them. Yet more relations who'd done some crazy shit.

I thought about one of my own decision points.

One summer night when I was sixteen, some friends and I were drinking beers and smoking cheap cigars in an abandoned parking lot. Suddenly, a big caravan of punks showed up, and they were looking to fight. We wore pegged pants and listened to New Order and the Cure. We weren't pussies, but we weren't looking for a brawl.

A short, stocky guy pulled his shirt off and slapped the cigar out of my friend's mouth. Then the one with an earring approached me quietly, watching my every move. He was measuring the right angle to clock me. This was it. I should have begged for mercy. He might have had a weapon.

I said, "Hey, calm down, man," and slammed my fist into his head. That surprised him. It was a direct hit, and he fell to the ground. He shrieked and grabbed his ear. I'd put his pretty little earring right into the side of his head. He looked up at me in fear, worried that I might punch him again.

We fought the rest of them off as best we could. I ended up with a black eye and a few bumps and bruises. It was one of the greatest nights of my life.

Confidence had always been my problem at work. Amidst org charts, best practices, and other bullshit, I'd lost my mojo. I had tried to stifle the crazy side of my personality that was associated with Flip Side. But it was also the source of my courage. Rather than risk acting out, I'd withdrawn completely, leaving only a shallow version of myself at work, exhibiting feeble abilities.

Flip Side was the reckless brother who loved me but kept fucking my life up. Now he said he could right all his past wrongs, if only I'd listen to him. He knew how to summon all the rage, the chips on our shoulder, the desperation of wanting to be ok. If I could do this one insane thing, he would save me. I'd have to give him control, but we could win it all.

"This time, I'm right!" he said.

I could see it. I could feel it. I was ready. Fuck them and fuck it. I went all in.

In the winter of 2017, over a period of weeks, I visited Wells Fargo three times. I transferred an increasing amount of dollars from our home equity line to Gemini. After each transfer, I went home and started buying ETH slowly so I didn't cause a run-up. I wanted to keep things quiet so I could accumulate in peace.

When it was all said and done, the debt on our line of credit exceeded $200,000. I bought 21,116 ETH that winter. Our average buy-in price was now $11.21. In total, we owned 26,750 ETH. Our total investment was more than $300,000.

In crypto, everyone talks about whales, the ones with the massive number of coins. They are a mythical force, making loads of money by knowing what's going to happen next. They move their huge stacks for maximum advantage while everyone else is in the dark. I always pictured them as Gordon

Gekko or Mr. Robot. A mix of tech billionaires and cold-blooded traders, with maybe a few Russian oligarchs thrown in. I don't think anyone thought it was a guy like me, sitting in his upstairs bedroom, buying more ETH than most people thought was prudent, then going downstairs and trying like hell to change the water filter in the refrigerator.

Eileen walked into the kitchen just as I was ready to give up with the filter. She started pouring the kids' milks for dinner.

"Well, we've done it," I said.

I saw an instant of terror in her eyes. When I worked for Eileen at Macromedia sixteen years before, she always seemed to know everything that was going on in her department, even if she only drifted into any particular meeting for a few minutes. She had that type of brain. But she didn't always let on that she did.

Later, I asked her if she had ever been nervous about the ETH investment. A strange question, since who wouldn't be, but one I needed to ask, considering her apparent complete lack of curiosity or concern during this period. She surprised me. She said that this was the only time she was actually afraid. But the other thing she sensed at that moment, which generated a more powerful feeling than the fear, was the fact that I was actually happy.

Despite my mania, I was happy, and that was good for the whole family. She didn't stop me from making this investment because she didn't want to break the spell I was under. That's a proof point to how miserable I'd been, how miserable I'd made her and the kids during my time at Acme and during my addict years. It's also evidence of her being slightly crazy herself because who would be willing to do that? She's obviously either a spiritual healer of unlimited power or a dangerous psychopath.

This was also the only time I fully let myself fathom what I'd done, how much of our future I'd bet on this thing that I'd only recently discovered. Going into debt by $200,000 was an absolutely reckless, insane thing to do. Even on r/EthTrader, filled with Pollyannas and true believers, I'd never heard of anyone going this big. Not even close. And in my real life, I hadn't ever heard of anyone, anywhere, who'd done something so crazy. I was a massive outlier. At most times, this just made me excited. But as we settled into our dinner routine, Eileen a bit quieter than usual, there was now an edge to my excitement.

CHAPTER NINETEEN

A NEW YEAR

A few days after Christmas 2016, Eileen and the kids headed to North Andover, Massachusetts, to visit her family for a week. That was impeccable timing, because I was able to attend the Blockchain Fintech Summit down the road in San Jose on January 3, 2017, without any normal-person obligations. The Summit was vaguely sponsored by the Chinese government, which was interested in crypto and had recently been showing up everywhere.

I had trouble sleeping those first days of 2017. I couldn't pull myself off crypto Twitter, r/EthTrader and *Coindesk* until late into the evening. I'd pop up a few hours later, wanting to get back online.

I parked my banged-up minivan with the dented passenger door on the roof parking lot of the San Jose Convention Center and sprinted fifty yards through the heaviest rainstorm I could remember. This was the first of three "atmospheric rivers" to drench Northern California that month. If these insane rains were an omen, I didn't know if I was doomed or blessed. I was now so immersed in the crypto world that I was flipping like a weather vane with speculation about the future, both hopeful and skeptical.

There in the distance, talking to a crowd of Chinese provincial bureaucrats, was a kindred spirit and one of my heroes, Andrew Keys, the chief evangelist of ConsenSys in Brooklyn. I'd heard him interviewed on a bunch of podcasts. I was a big fan of his company.

For an ETH freak like me, ConsenSys was the hippest, edgiest, most profoundly cool company in the world. They called themselves an Ethereum Production Studio, and they ran the company as a holacracy, meaning it was structured as a flat organization, unlike a traditional corporation. Its founder, Joseph Lubin, was an early disciple of Ethereum and a mentor to Vitalik on the business side. He was a co-founder who helped Vitalik get the word out and attract developers to Ethereum after it launched in 2015.

As a professional prophet, Keys traveled the world, extolling the virtues of Ethereum. Now I was with him as he talked to this group of squares in suits and ties. He was sweating and effusive, sharing the gospel, telling them how Ethereum would change everything, doling out proof points like a street-corner preacher: warehouses full of developers in the Philippines, a major recording artist interested in the Ethereum-based music dApp Ujo, big corporations quietly turning to Ethereum in an effort to become more flat. Halle—fucking—lujah. This was my dream scenario for this conference. I didn't want to hear about Guangdong Province's leadership in some bullshit state-sponsored attempt by the Chinese government to monopolize blockchain. I wanted to hear how fully decentralized Ethereum was going to take over the world.

Finally Andrew had to leave, but before he did, I got my two minutes. I confessed my story, how I'd left Acme, how I was committed to Ethereum, how my mission was to do PR for crypto projects and advance decentralization. And could he arrange an interview at ConsenSys for me to be considered for work as a PR consultant? "Yes, brother," he said. "I'll hook you up."

I met other brothers and sisters that day. We were members of the crypto diaspora. We spoke in shorthand about our mental condition, investments, and plans to somehow work in crypto full time. At lunch I sat down with a group of Indian tech guys, and we just bonded and blathered on. We'd all glimpsed something that most other people hadn't seen, and we were comfortable speaking about it in each other's presence.

Finding crypto isn't like joining a new company and sending a polite little fart of an update to your LinkedIn connections. It is a civil disturbance. It is a whole new belief system. That's why asking someone when they went down the rabbit hole is like asking them when they found God. It is a full religious conversion, not a lateral move.

Once the seed germinates, Ethereum in particular doesn't let you go. Before long, it is impossible to get excited about anything in the traditional economy. The Ethereum Vampire Effect (EVE) is real. Once you get it, all you want to do is suck the blood out of every centralized entity that crosses your path.

Magical thinking aside, I still had to make money in the traditional economy, and that meant revisiting the ghosts of my Acme execution in the form of the public relations firm Acme set me up with to secure my departure. Even though I wanted to say goodbye to the world of lobbyists and public relations-types who'd rejected me, I still had to pay the bills. Revenue from BitGo, my one crypto client, wasn't enough. Plus, we now had to buy our own health insurance, which cost $2,400 per month. And, of course, there were the extravagant family vacations I'd agreed to in return for being allowed to put everything we had, plus $200,000 of debt, into ETH. The monthly payment on that debt ensured I wouldn't forget.

I needed this Acme-assisted account for the money, even though it provided an unpleasant glimpse of my miserable future if crypto didn't turn out to be a viable career path. I reported to two people during my service, initially a woman who was smart and considered me an ally in firm dynamics, which I had no interest in. Then, when she left, an ambitious mid-level man on the rise who had little regard for me, not necessarily because he was an asshole, but because I was of no consequence. A forty-five-year-old corporate cast-off was of little use to an ambitious up-and-comer. I know, I'm a bitter old man. Maybe I'm ageist because I don't want to be reporting to someone twenty years younger than me. But I don't want to.

After editing a simple document for one of their clients several times in an attempt to manage competing visions of the project, I knew the dystopia that awaited if crypto dried up. We'd lose our investment and my crypto clients. Then I'd become a resume-carrying member of the Weird Old Fuckers Club I pitied back at Acme. I'd have to learn to brownnose junior staffers and get used to being kicked around by younger animals who didn't respect freaky old silverbacks who never made alpha.

So to say I was excited about my upcoming video interview with ConsenSys would be an understatement. I wanted another big-name crypto client, and I wanted something squarely in the Ethereum world. I also needed the money.

Andrew was true to his word and hooked me up with someone at ConsenSys HQ. We agreed on a time for a video conference.

Like pretty much everyone in my professional world, it seemed, this person was in their mid-twenties. I found a local newspaper clip of them starring on their high school lacrosse team around the same time I became concerned my pee stream was weakening. But hey, crypto transcended barriers. A person's passion for it was more important than age, I thought.

I got myself all dolled up in a collared shirt and sat on our upstairs couch with the blue-painted wall as background, waiting for our video conference. The agreed-upon time came and went. I still sat there, now with a forlorn look on my face. Poor old bastard.

I emailed them. They referenced some confusion about the time. Ok, shit happens. I'm sure they were busy. The important thing was that we ended up connecting. We set a new time, and, like *Groundhog Day*, I was ready to flash my prettiest smile in my best collared shirt, sitting on the couch in front of the perfect blue background. This time, they joined as scheduled. Briefly.

As our likenesses came into focus, we took a look at each other. Then we said hello. I was just about to launch into my spiel when they said, "Oh, shoot, I just realized that I have another appointment I need to be at. Dan, I'm sorry, I'm going to have to reschedule."

I stared on, the hurt eyes of a man picked last at kickball by his own brother. "No problem."

I was outraged and crushed. I wondered if I was fooling myself that I could make a living in crypto. Was I delusional?

Since I'd won BitGo as a client, I'd been optimistic. But maybe it was a fluke. A troubling possibility I tried not to think about.

As January turned to February 2017, life continued with its normal pace and family obligations. Each day was a routine mix of making snacks, driving the kids to after-school activities and sports practices and paying bills. Lots of bills. There were tutors, speech therapists, new winter coats, and dental visits with no insurance, to name a few.

When I told Eileen that we needed to be careful with spending, she assured me that we were spending the bare minimum. I didn't have the will to fight about it, especially since I didn't want to shine a light on the fact that our ETH was still significantly underwater. Plus the blood oath I had sworn, which allowed me to gamble our entire future in the first place, restricted me from complaining about the high cost of our upcoming trips. Like the drunk and the girl in *Leaving Las Vegas*, we'd get along fine as long as neither of us acknowledged the elephant in the room: we were on our way to financial ruin.

CHAPTER TWENTY

SPRING FEVER

The first stop in our Kamikaze Live While You Can World Tour was Puerto Vallarta during the February 2017 school break. Unfortunately, we picked a terrible resort in a beautiful location. The food was decorative yet disgusting. A typical dish was a radish filled with mayonnaise-y sauce, wrapped in a wilted piece of spinach, poked with a toothpick. A whole platter full. Right next to stew meat labeled "filet mignon."

The sun was getting to me, so I left the pool and went back to the room for a break. I was trying to stay away from my phone, because the price of ETH was depressing, and I could easily lose several hours on r/EthTrader if I wasn't careful. But I couldn't help myself—I never could—so I checked.

ETH was going up. My crypto app animated the price in real time. Sell orders were quickly gobbled up by buy orders, which made the price flash green rather than red. What had previously been a red flame of hell was now lighting up like a Christmas tree. This was amazing. I kept watching, and it kept going up, passing $13.50 on February 25th.

Just like that, our investment had gone from being way down to up $60,000. I pulled myself away from my phone and briskly walked back to the pool. Eileen asked me where

I'd been. I told her that our ETH investment was in the black, *and we'd made enough money to pay for our vacations* (not quite, but I wanted to make a point).

The rest of that trip was a blur of disgusting food, sunburns, and ETH ascending. Every time I checked my phone, the price was higher. The restaurants didn't have good WiFi, so I didn't bring my phone to dinner. Invariably, when we got back to the room a couple of hours later, we were up thousands of dollars.

For months, I'd tried to convince myself that the crashing ETH price was only a paper loss and that the flashing red numbers on my phone weren't important, even though they represented the verdict on the biggest bet of my life. I had been telling myself that we were in the long game, even if that was only partially true. Now that momentum was turning in my favor, at least for the time being, cognitive dissonance made it hard to believe it was real. Deep down, I'd had the strongest conviction I'd ever had that ETH would pay off, but watching it rise like a phoenix before my eyes was like seeing Santa Claus in the flesh.

The r/EthTrader boards were starting to pop. Every hour, it seemed, a hundred new people joined. These were noobs who were hoping to jump on right before the rocket ship took off. We welcomed them—we welcomed everybody—and we noticed that the trolls had gone away. The short sellers and haters who piled on the FUD in a bear market disappeared in a puff of black smoke the moment the price went up.

I couldn't fully participate in the delirium because I was still in Mexico. But I was keeping close tabs. Eileen quickly decided she didn't give a shit about this magic money if it meant the rest of our family vacation focused around me relating snippets of something Vitalik said or a prediction of future riches based on the analysis of a fellow r/EthTrader.

I'd volunteer to go to the gift shop and buy the bottled water. I'd offer to go down to the lobby and make dinner reservations for our next disgusting meal. It usually took me longer than expected, though, because I'd buy a pack of Marlboro Reds. I don't smoke. I'd have a cigarette while walking around that crappy resort with the million-dollar views. I couldn't help feeling like I was in a Polo ad, that this might be my life if the price kept rising like I thought it would. I'd be in linen and thousand-dollar shades, rich as hell.

On our last day, I ordered fajitas from a self-service buffet. The handles of the spoons used to scoop raw ingredients were sticky with chicken juice. I woke up at two a.m., foaming at the mouth like a dying animal. I couldn't stop puking. It was so bad that I took a taxi into downtown Puerto Vallarta in the middle of the night to buy Dramamine. None of it mattered. I distinctly remember trying not to puke, looking down at my phone and watching ETH surpass $14, a big psychological barrier at the time. We were up $75,000. My body was sick, but my soul was dancing. What I thought would happen with Ethereum might just be happening.

Ironically, the catalyst for this price rise was a sudden interest in Ethereum from corporations, governments, and other centralized institutions. Back in New York, they'd announced a new organization, spearheaded by Ethereum veterans, called the Enterprise Ethereum Alliance. There were thirty-five initial members, including some of the largest corporations in the world: Microsoft, J.P. Morgan, and British Petroleum. Over a day-long webcast conference at the J.P. Morgan office, they expressed their belief in Ethereum and sketched out working groups to aid development and interoperability with private chains. This is the thing Andrew Keys had hinted at in San Jose. The markets were responding. Blockchain *might* actually work, and Ethereum *might* actually be the winning platform.

There was a flurry of mainstream press. Most articles were similar to the one in *Fortune* ("Big Business Giants from J.P. Morgan to Microsoft are Getting Behind Ethereum"), which described how corporations were starting to recognize the cost savings and efficiencies Ethereum made possible. But it wasn't punk rock. They intended to take the guts of the blockchain and discard its decentralized soul. This would allow them to retain control and set the rules, creating private chains. While these private chains might someday be connected to the uncurated public Ethereum chain, my feeling then and now is that they are underestimating the power of this movement. Corporations aren't going to be able to control the path of disruption when blockchain really takes off. They are going to be extremely uncomfortable at some point in the future. But at that moment, God bless them, their interest was legitimizing Ethereum in a big way.

Our taxi arrived at the Puerto Vallarta airport, and a hot blast of air hit me as I opened the door and prepared for the travel ordeal ahead. I willed myself to check the price, even though I felt like I might pass out. ETH was at $15.50. We were up more than $100,000.

It scared me that this might just be the beginning. We had so much invested that even a small rise was big money. There was a pit in my stomach that told me something much bigger could happen, and it might change our lives. Was I ready for that? Was this real? Was this investment going to alter space and time, like in *Back to the Future*?

This wasn't supposed to be happening to me. And while it made me nervous, it felt so damn good. But it was new territory, and I needed a new way to cope. The mental tools I'd used to grit my way through my career, and also since betting big on crypto after losing my job—self-deprecation, an ability to grind, and a burning resentment at the man—were inadequate for helping me process this new feeling.

Flip Side would usually sabotage me at this point, even though he sent me down this path. He ruled through impulse fuck-ups. But now the die was cast, and he was unable to stop it.

As I suffered in line while we waited to get on the plane home from Mexico, ETH kept going. It was a beautiful girl who'd fallen in love with me. When I rubbed my eyes, her sweet smile was always there to greet me. I was sick as a dog, extremely dehydrated. I refused to talk to airport personnel or anyone in line. A group of nice older ladies next to us were all jazzed up about their trip. They struck up a conversation with Eileen as we waited for customs. I avoided them all until I needed to hand something to Eileen. The ladies were shocked and disgusted. They whispered, "He's with you?"

I was sick. I didn't want to puke, and I didn't know if I could survive my headache with all of the delays on each end of international travel. But I was also shedding something on that flight. That failed professional was saying goodbye—at least for awhile—because all evidence, for the time being, pointed to my having made a very good move.

When I finally recovered a few days later, ETH hadn't slowed down. On March 4, 2017, as I lay on the couch drinking Gatorade and binge-watching *Narcos* on Netflix, I was feeling damned good.

On March 11, ETH passed $20. We were up more than $200,000.

This was life-changing. If ETH just held, we'd be ok. I kept playing with the idea of having that amount of money at my disposal. It could pay for college for at least one, maybe two of the kids. If everything just stopped right there and I cashed out, I'd consider this the greatest professional thing I'd ever done.

But that wasn't the goal. We were going all the way, wherever that led.

***

Three weeks later, as I prepared to head to the blockchain-focused Chamber of Digital Commerce Conference in Washington, D.C., on March 15, 2017, on BitGo business, I was ecstatic. I was excited to be among my crypto people. Best of all, it was taking place at my alma mater, Georgetown University.

I'd only been back to Georgetown once since college, and it was during a miserable time at Acme when I was in town to kiss the hand of a new master. This time was different. That man skipping around with rainbows and unicorns shooting out his ass? That was me! I chatted up various student workers in the bistro. I visited all of my old dorms, asking kids to remove their headphones so I could tell them, "I used to live here!" I read every flier in the student union. It looked like there were a hell of a lot of great activities scheduled! Every time I checked the price of ETH, I was richer.

I walked the streets at night, strolling shamelessly through the lobbies of the hotels I used to stay at. An opioid-like coma enveloped me in a wave of good moods. Everything seemed so pleasant.

I woke up the next morning and walked the whole way to campus in a blizzard. The expression on my face was one of psychotic happiness. When I finally arrived at the conference, I handed my jacket to the attendant at the door, picked up my name tag and turned my attention to the assembled group. It was a mix of business types, government officials, and a smattering of Bitcoin and Ethereum veterans.

The Tapscotts kicked things off with an opening presentation. They were a father/son duo who'd recently published the book *Blockchain Revolution*. They were trying to establish themselves as leaders of the Blockchain Intelligentsia. They'd done a lot to evangelize blockchain, but I couldn't help but be annoyed at their keynote-ready personas. From the stage, they announced a new institute where monied interests could learn about this new world. With assistance from the Tapscotts, anyone could master it.

Don Tapscott said something like, "This will be the first world-class blockchain salon." His forehead was perspiring from the heat of the spotlight. "You will be hearing more about this initiative from Alex Tapscott, later in the day."

The Tapscotts were tight with Perianne Boring, the head of the Chamber of Digital Commerce, a blockchain advocacy organization she founded. I was curious to see her in person. I'd followed her closely online. She was a member of the lobbyist class in D.C. By all accounts, she'd worked her ass off to get this group off the ground, and for that, she should be applauded. But I'd heard her on the underground *Bitcoin Uncensored* podcast. She'd been ambushed with a more substantive interview than she expected. She revealed herself to be shockingly blockchain illiterate. She seemed to think that ACH bank transfers were a type of blockchain, which is pretty much the most embarrassing and blasphemous thing one could say. That, along with her continual references to "innovation," made me think that she thought blockchain was simply the next big thing, a perfect opportunity to build an organization with her as the head, rather than something that would shake the power structure. Her lawyer sent a cease and desist letter, unsuccessfully trying to prevent the podcast from airing.

During the morning break, I made my way near the stage and extended my hand to meet her. Hi, Perianne, I'm Dan Conway. I'm here with BitGo. Nice to meet you."

"Oh, hi, Dan, I'm glad you could make it."

She was turning to move on, but I couldn't resist. I leaned in with a smile on my face, which caught her by surprise. At that moment, on that day, my eyes were those of a demented child. I felt the urge to say something unexpected. "Your interview on that podcast was pretty wild."

She knew exactly what I was talking about. The incident hadn't been widely reported, but I was all over everything blockchain. Nothing escaped my attention. This sounded more like a threat than an act of compassion. I was like a villain in a movie who turns to a mother in mortal danger, strokes the hair of her five-year-old daughter and says, "Such a lovely girl."

Now I had her attention. She looked back into my pupils, dilated with mania and money and greed and joy.

"Oh, yeah, you heard that? Uh … thanks."

"Yes, I did." That was all I had to say about that.

I was obviously a creep. She pulled away and moved on to say hello to a pair of Price Waterhouse consultants.

The Chamber was building a structure around blockchain comprised of the same monied interests the Tapscotts were courting—the IBMs, Accentures, and Visas of the world. I wanted to tear shit down, not build a community that rewarded the same douchebag behavior from corporate America. For that reason, I preferred the nerds across town at the competing advocacy organization Coin Center for blockchain lobbying and communications. They had a different funding structure and were more grounded in cypherpunk ethos.

But the story of the minute, hour, and day at the conference was Ethereum. As a truly disruptive, unneutered, decentralized, and open-source platform, it was exponentially more interesting than the blockchain-light projects promoted by the wannabe gatekeepers at this event.

I sat in the back. I noticed a familiar face a few rows in front of me. God bless him, there was Andrew Keys. He was doing what we were all doing—checking the price of ETH. After taking a quick look at the charts, he'd put his phone away and try to focus on what was being said on stage. But a minute or two later, he'd take another look.

The same sequence repeated itself with other attendees all over the room, all day long. It was like that scene from *The Big Short* when the Bear Stearns CEO was on stage in the early days of the 2008 financial crisis, telling everyone there was nothing to worry about while Bear's stock price plummeted, setting off alerts on everyone's BlackBerries. Except we were experiencing the opposite. As the Tapscotts droned on, a new, uncurated asset was being created before our very eyes, like a skyscraper being constructed at one hundred times normal speed. We were witnessing the dawn of a new day, the ascension of the Ethereum blockchain and its launch into public consciousness. We were going to change the world and get rich, not necessarily in that order. Who could blame us for being distracted?

On the evening of March 16, I sat on my plane at Reagan Airport, preparing to takeoff on my way back to San Francisco. I took one last look at the price. ETH crossed $35. We were up $600,000. When I landed six hours later, I powered up my phone. Now ETH was at $47. We were up nearly $1 million. Holy fuck.

Something called the flywheel effect was making the price of ETH rise. As the price went up, more and more people were buying, decreasing price resistance. Like a crowd of people going through a turnstile, new investors were pushing price resistance until all resistance was practically nonexistent.

As the price increased, the misfits, high stakes gamblers, and Ethereum true believers I'd been spending time with on r/EthTrader became a family. We'd suffered together through the dark days, licking our wounds and professing our continued belief in decentralization and Ethereum. We'd ignored the abuse from Bitcoin maximalists and other trolls who had invaded our homes to spread fear, uncertainty, and doubt with comments such as, Goodbye, Ethereum, you guys are idiots! We'd endured the herd of suits on CNBC telling us crypto was an illusion, a fever dream, a fad.

We'd also dealt with the skeptics in our real lives. For example, one Sunday night in December 2016, when ETH was tanking, I was supposed to go to a party. I ended up not being able to make it. One of the moms, an acquaintance and a real card, raised her voice and said, "Where's Dan ... *working on the blockchain?*"

Everyone had a big laugh.

Some r/EthTraders sold their coins during the downturn and left, but most of us flashed our HODL signs—a crypto meme signaling one's intention to hold—and kept our chins up. Now, we were together during this historic rise. Our faith had been rewarded. This was life-changing money for most of us, and it was emotional. *I love you guys!* was a common post during late-night rallies, and we meant it.

We developed our own euphoric subculture. An early Ethereum believer and elementary school teacher from Kansas popularized the "Donut Day" meme by posting pictures of donuts being served at his school. Subsequently, every thirteen-dollar rise was deemed Donut Day. When newcomers to the thread asked how high we thought ETH would go, we'd all respond, *Bout Tree Fiddy.* We talked about buying Lambos, but most of us were kidding. We'd comment, *This is gentlemen* when the price suddenly shot up. I don't know why. College kids were skipping class to watch the charts. We'd cheer them on and then remind them to get back to their schoolwork. A trader called Science Guy made screwball price predictions. After he returned from a brief trip, someone wrote, *Welcome back, you filthy animal. Your technical analysis is shit, but it wouldn't be r/EthTrader without you.*

When you're making money and spending time with those you love, it's all good.

We felt entitled to a little fun after white-knuckling it for so long. The popular press of the time chose to profile the most obnoxious and lizardy among us, those shirtless tools who flaunted their wealth and were soon ready to jump into the next coin, hoping for another trip to the moon. But r/EthTrader was grounded in true believers. There were many others like me—improbable zealots who didn't get in because they were looking to be cool. We bought into the vision of a decentralized world. I'm sure there were a fair number of people like me who could get lost in enthusiasm and be self-destructive, but that didn't matter. Because it looked like we were right.

That we could get rich by putting our money where our mouth was wasn't a flaw but a feature. I wouldn't have been able or willing to fund Ethereum's development by buying ETH if it had been a nonprofit with no financial upside for me. But since there was a possibility of changing our financial fate by buying ETH, something we believed in on its merits, the incentive was there for us to fund this network. Us. Not the venture capitalists who dominated Silicon Valley. Not the accredited investors who are already Masters of the Universe. But common Joes like me, who found their way here through a lifetime of struggle and chose to bet on something that could benefit us and make the world a better place.

J.T. Nichol, the forty-something elementary school teacher from Kansas, believed the Ethereum token could help at-risk high school kids in his classes track their academic obligations and progress even when they switched schools.

Steven was a mid-level corporate warrior in a so-called glamorous job who traveled all over the world, preventing any semblance of a family life. He tracked ETH from Bologna to Saudi Arabia. When finally he was spit out and fired from his job, all he had left was his ETH and a dream to control his own destiny.

Tracy was a thirty-six-year-old man working for a shady insurance company. He was fired from his job not long after placing the first-ever crypto risk into the Lloyd's of London insurance market. That was apparently too shady. Soon, he put up his own shingle.

Ryan was a fifty-seven-year-old libertarian who grew up in a large family where the family motto was, "Don't hurt people and don't take people's stuff." Crypto in general and Ethereum in particular was a way to make this platitude actionable.

John was a thirty-four-year-old with a soul-deadening job as an assistant procurement manager. He and his new wife lived in a small and expensive apartment at the edge of Silicon Valley, struggling with student loans. They wanted to have a baby, but how could they afford it and still pay the bills? He invested in the Ethereum crowdsale anyway after immersing himself in the technology for months.

Pelayo was a twenty-two-year-old man living with his fifty-four-year-old mother in Brazil. Hyperinflation and corrupt government policies depleted their already-meager savings. Then his father left in the middle of the night, taking all of their remaining money. Pelayo read that Ethereum couldn't be gamed by the power elites. He scraped together the money for a mining rig and earned thousands of ETH when it was priced at less than one dollar.

Call us douchebags if you like, but we were more than just degenerate gamblers playing roulette and dreaming of Lambos. We were caught up in something bigger than ourselves.

CHAPTER TWENTY-ONE

FINANCIAL EMERGENCY

I listened to loud music on my headphones while walking the dog. I imagined myself as the star of each song. The mashup of images that ran through my head involved me being worshipped. I'd put on a big bash for all of my friends to celebrate Ethereum. I'd be on stage. Right when everyone was at full throttle, drunk as hell (except for me), ranting and raving in ecstasy at something I said, I'd point to stage right, and out would come the Smiths, or Jane's Addiction, or a similar awesome band, who'd start jamming right into their biggest hits and my favorite songs. Sometimes it was "Jane Says" or "Cemetery Gates." One time it was "Centerfold" by J.Geils Band, which is an odd choice for a mosh pit celebration song, but hey, it was my daydream.

I'd been posting articles on Medium about cryptocurrency throughout 2015 and 2016. Now that crypto was in the news, friends and acquaintances began asking me about it. With big profits in my sales, I was more confident than ever explaining why I thought ETH was going to be huge and why it was still a good investment.

I'd tell them right off the bat that I was a true believer, that I didn't know what would happen, that if they invested they needed to be ok with losing it all. "Of course," they'd say.

With that stale preamble out of the way, I'd move in for the kill. It was simply in my nature to explain Ethereum in a way that convinced people to invest. I fully believed it was the right thing to do. And now, with a million dollars of "I was right" profits backing me up, I was like an athlete who had suddenly hit his stride. Flip Side, the guy who wanted glory and fame, was satisfied as hell and didn't mess with me.

I'd charm them with anecdotes from my own story, I'd explain my thinking about the future, I'd tell them the amount of time I'd spent researching crypto, I'd explain the smoking gun of developers moving to Ethereum. I'd do it nearly without blinking, entrancing them with all the confidence a human can muster.

It wasn't my intention to go around getting people to buy ETH. I would still have given those lectures even if someone told me they'd never invest. I just needed to express it. I was compelled to tell them about this life-changing thing that was not only a once-in-a-generation investment opportunity but a technology that would transform the world in the coming decades.

I got a sense of what it was like to be a prophet.

I was once again like Chris McCandless from *Into the Wild,* who gave up society and traveled the country as a hobo. His spiritual experience came when he was flat broke, living off the land, and the kindness of strangers. Mine came when I'd become rich and no longer needed the kindness of strangers.

My baby boomer tax accountant who started off our annual meeting by trying to convince me to sell did an about-face after our discussion. I helped him sign up to an exchange. He said he was in for $10,000. He called the next day to say he settled on $20,000. Seven members of my family invested, including my eighty-six-year-old mother, who white-knuckled her wire transfer hoping it would go through a day early so she could capture more of those sweet gains. Everyone around the country, my brothers and sisters on r/EthTrader, were having these same conversations, spreading the word, compounding interest in Ethereum and accelerating the rise in value of ETH through the law of supply and demand.

The mainstream press was paying attention to Ethereum for the first time in a big way. Outlets like CNBC introduced ETH to a whole new set of investors with articles like the one on May 24, 2017, that blared, "Bitcoin may have more than doubled this year, but rival Ethereum is up 2,000 percent. Here's why."

I started acting differently, and Eileen was concerned. I'd take walks with a hoodie over my head and a blank look on my face. She noticed that I was having a hard time focusing on things like doing the dishes and cleaning up the dog shit in the backyard. I tried to tell her that our lives were changing, but she didn't want to hear it. She didn't like change. And she had compartmentalized this whole thing. She didn't want to think about it.

Now, after the kids were asleep, I'd offer to help her fold the laundry. Normally this meant I was interested in having a romantic experience. My next suggestion would be, "Hey, do you want a massage?" But these days I'd say something like, "Hey, Bitcoin is struggling with capacity, and that means a lot of people are going long on ETH."

She considered all of this crypto talk a form of nonsense babble that she had to endure from her eccentric, but thankfully sober, husband. If I'd told her that crypto turned out to be make-believe like the World Wrestling Foundation, she wouldn't have been the least bit surprised. But now she was getting sick of all the nonstop talk. To her, it was like I was saying, "Hey, Mighty Mouse invited me over, and he's going to cook half of Rumpelstiltskin's mustache for dinner. Isn't that nice, baby?"

She had a hard time coming up with meaningful responses to the gibberish. She couldn't humor me anymore, so she told me to please shut up, at least for a little while, about ETH.

Things were getting tense, until I had an idea. I told her that for Mother's Day, I'd like to take the five of us to see *Hamilton* in San Francisco. The show had sold out in twenty minutes months before. It was the hottest ticket in town, with seats selling for three hundred dollars a pop on the secondary market. In any previous version of our lives, there was no way we'd consider going. Cryptocurrency would pay for this phenomenal family experience. Eileen was thrilled.

But I realized we needed some help figuring out how to deal with our new state of play. The decisions we needed to make would shape the direction of our lives for the rest of our lives, and I wanted Eileen engaged and on board. I also needed some conventional thinking to temper my enthusiasm before I spun off the earth's axis.

On April 28, 2017, ETH crossed sixty-four dollars. We were up $1.4 million.

That morning, I received an email from Sean, a friend of ours who owned a midsize financial advisory firm. Our sons were friends. Eileen and I adored the whole family.

I'd previously confided in him about our investment in ETH. Since then, he'd boned up on crypto. I'd made the decision to have our money managed at his firm at some point in the future. I said I'd be in touch to schedule a meeting. Now he'd beaten me to the punch.

The subject of his email was *Financial Emergency*. He said he'd clear his calendar to meet with us that day if we could make it. Eileen looked relieved when I told her about the meeting. Sean's the kind of guy you want to have custody of your children if you are killed in a head-on collision. His good judgment and maturity might be just what we needed.

"Hi Dan, hi Eileen!" Sean was looking bright and cheery. "There are coffee and muffins in the conference room. I'll be there in a minute."

I wouldn't have minded a muffin. I knew Sean wouldn't have one. Whenever we went out to dinner with him and his wife Cathy, I noticed he never ate too much. When depressed, I could consume a dozen Krispy Kremes and two containers of whole milk.

We settled into the conference room and waited for Sean and his director of wealth management. It was a crisp spring morning, and the view from the window looking over the San Francisco Bay was beautiful.

I looked over at Eileen, who was looking at the big screen. The title of the first page of the presentation was *Conway Wealth Management Plan*. That had a nice ring to it. Eileen looked dazed, and I think this was the first time she realized that our lives might be changing.

Pleasantries dispensed, Sean got to the point.

"Dan, I want to compliment you on identifying ETH and having the guts to invest in it. It's up six hundred percent in the last three months. I've never seen anything like this in my twenty years in finance."

I nodded and took a slug of coffee, which was still piping hot. "The good news is that it still has a lot of room to run," I said.

"I won't presume to tell you about ETH, because you know way more about it than me, Dan. But what I can tell you is that no matter what the asset is, after a rise like this, the price could drop precipitously, simply because it has gone up too fast. I've worked with many people over the years who got half of a trade right—buying low—but then blew the second half by not selling because they didn't want to miss the top."

I leaned forward and laced my fingers in front of me on the table. I wanted Sean and Eileen to know he had my full respectful attention. While Sean was speaking, I remembered the famous quote from Bernard Baruch, the Wall Street financier, who said, "I made my money by selling too soon." That made sense in theory, but he didn't own any ETH.

Each of Sean's data points and anecdotes were making the case that selling at least a big chunk, maybe half or more, was the prudent thing to do. "Early in my career, during the dot com bust, I saw a couple in their forties watch the value of their Cisco stock decline from $7 million to $900,000," he said. "They were going to retire, but they ended up having to keep working."

Eileen was nodding. I didn't blame her. He was making a lot of sense. This was actually what I wanted to happen in that meeting, a little cold water dumped on my burning-hot euphoria. Selling a big chunk seemed like the smart thing to do. But while I had been looking forward to this meeting, it had been like looking forward to exercise. Now I didn't feel like going to the gym.

"I'm willing to sell some. I think that would be smart. But, honestly, things are just getting started. The biggest conference of the year, Consensus, in New York, is happening in a couple of weeks."

Regardless of trading patterns and financial psychology, in spite of economic history, my reasoning told me that ETH was going much higher, and soon. I noticed my voice speeding up. I tried to slow it back down and verbalize my thoughts in crisp bullet points. "Everything's coming together. Mainstream interest is starting to pick up. Consensus could spark an even bigger rally."

But I was here to be reasonable, to a point. I leaned back in my chair and asked Eileen a question. "How about we sell enough to get our entire investment out and to pay the taxes if ETH crosses $125? If ETH falls to $30, we'll do the same thing. That will cost us more ETH, but either way, we can't lose." I wasn't worried in the least about ETH dropping to $30, because I was confident it was still going up.

Sean jumped in. "Eileen, you said paying for the kids' college education is a priority. Dan, are you sure you don't want to sell more now to lock that up?"

"Yeah, maybe we should do that, Dan?" Eileen was deferring to me. A right I felt I had earned, considering the performance of this investment so far. That felt good.

"Guys, I've been watching this so closely, I have a good sense of what is going to happen next. I'm up for taking more out if it goes beyond $125, but I'm positive we should just focus on a plan for getting our initial investment out right now."

Of course, no one knows what's going to happen next with an investment, but I didn't care, because I felt I did. I had raised my voice a little bit and was trying to contain the emotion I was feeling.

"Sean, we made this investment because we wanted to become financially independent. The goal is to not have to work anymore, not just to make a chunk of money for our nest egg."

I'd tried to discuss this with Eileen before, but she never seemed to hear me. But now she knew that I meant it. Everyone in the room knew I meant it. I wasn't going to go full-rational when this moment required us to continue going rogue.

"Eileen, are you ok with this?" I asked.

I thought she might be mad, but she wasn't. She seemed satisfied to have a plan that meant we wouldn't end up any worse than when we started. "Ok, as long as we stick to our plan to get our money out if it starts dropping."

"Absolutely."

We turned back towards Sean and the team, who'd been watching this marital moment play out in front of them. "OK, we have a plan," Sean said. He started gathering his papers together. He looked satisfied. After a few minutes of small talk in the lobby, we thanked everyone and headed for the elevators.

We had a plan that would protect the upside of what I considered the greatest investment opportunity of a generation, perhaps in the history of the world.

***

At Sean's recommendation, we engaged a new CPA based down the road in San Jose. He knew a lot about stock options and things like that, so I assumed crypto taxes would be more in his wheelhouse.

He greeted us as we walked through his office door.

"Hello, Conways!" He was of African descent, and his voice sounded like God's. We liked him immediately.

For thirty minutes, we told him our story and explained our financial picture. He seemed to be a really great guy and shared our values. We exchanged stories about our kids. Then he got to his punch line.

"Well, Sean briefed me. And I've been doing my own research. I can tell you that crypto is mainly used for money laundering. I'd recommend that you get out of this investment at your earliest opportunity."

Oh, boy, he was one of those. Eileen looked shaken, but this was music to my ears. It was another proof point that most people still had no idea about what crypto was. There was still room for crypto to run up in price while the mainstream caught up. Crypto was for real. Ethereum was going to change the world. Maybe not tomorrow, but someday.

CHAPTER TWENTY-TWO

SUMMER DREAMS AND ICO MADNESS

I n the spring of 2017, Blockchain was becoming a big deal, and I saw a business opportunity. I decided to put Zealot Communications on steroids, hire a full team, rent an office space and prepare to take on a bunch of new clients. The goal was to become the number-one crypto/blockchain PR firm in the world. We'd be a big platform and help the industry's most important projects.

My LinkedIn profile would be gloriously reborn with some Jedi-sounding crypto skills and knowledge. People at Acme had been looking at my profile. I wished I could be there when they read my new career headline: *Prophet of Decentralization.*

In this new mega-firm, I'd primarily manage the employees, since Eileen preferred to continue working from our kitchen table. I'd start by finding some post-collegiate millennials and teach them the ropes. An image of me addressing a couple of new employees entered my mind. I'd make a joke, then insist, "JUST KIDDING!"

I wondered how long it would take until those little fuckers made fun of me behind my back. I pictured me leading a study session on cryptocurrency and blockchain. How many times would I say the same thing a different way while still not properly explaining the concept before they tuned me out?

Would they earn their keep? I'd have to create some systems and weekly reports to track their productivity. Would they try to start their own shop and steal my clients? I'd keep an eye on them and guard my relationships. Would I have to throw a holiday party and invite their partners for an evening together when I'd rather be at home eating some cornbread and chili? I'd be the boss, so I'd better dust off the Santa outfit.

There were reminders in the real world that I might not be cut out to be a big shot PR consultant. I'd had the opportunity months earlier to meet with the marketing team at a16z, a leading venture capital firm headed by Marc Andreessen. I'd gotten the meeting by reaching out to Cindy, a colleague at a past job. At the time, I was one of the few PR people pitching myself as dedicated to crypto/blockchain.

The meeting went well, and now with crypto popping and the media paying attention, a16z recommended me to someone in their network. His name was Olaf Carson Wee, the first Coinbase employee. Olaf had left Coinbase to start Polychain Capital, one of the first and most-prominent crypto hedge funds. Olaf was a super sharp guy. I admired him for his broad and mature perspective on the future of crypto. He'd soon be on the cover of *Fortune*. He emailed me and wanted to talk. I was totally thrilled—this was the type of client that could make our business.

The conversation started off well, and I believe he could tell that I knew this space and had a passion for it. He explained that a number of crypto projects his fund had invested in, many built on the Ethereum blockchain, would need help with marketing and communications. Could he send them my way? Umm, yes. That's what I should have said and then gotten off the phone. But during our final minutes of small talk before we said goodbye, he mentioned Cindy and said how much he had enjoyed working with her. My nervous energy and perhaps disbelief that I was going to be a big player in crypto sent words to my mouth that completely surprised me. "Yes, Cindy and I have done great work together."

No, we hadn't. I'd never worked on a project with her. There seemed to be a pause on the line, and then we finally said goodbye.

I imagine that before calling me, he'd gotten the skinny from a16z, which was probably something like, "He seems like he knows what he's talking about. He and Cindy worked at the same firm many years ago, but we haven't worked with him, so see what you think."

I never heard from Olaf again.

I also met with the folks at Dfinity Labs. They were getting ready to launch a new blockchain that was complementary and somewhat competitive to Ethereum. These guys were the real deal, with serious computer science and crypto credentials. Especially Dominic Williams, who was in the Vitalik-echelon of original blockchain thinkers and made sure I knew it. While I believed Ethereum would dominate the smart contract space, I also believed there was room for other breakthroughs, and if anyone was going to pull it off, these guys were contenders.

I met them at a house in Palo Alto that they were using as an office. We talked for an hour, half in the kitchen while coffee was being made, half on bean bags in the living room. An assistant took detailed notes as I talked, which was flattering but a little unnerving, because I didn't want them to steal my approach and do it themselves. Following the meeting, I sent them a proposal that included the two bolded lines below that will go down in infamy:

*One area of focus that I think should start now is advancing Dominic himself as one of the blockchain visionaries beyond the crypto sphere. My brain is still ringing after our discussion in the kitchen on Friday. **I recall that scene from** Good Will Hunting **where that professor says he is one of a handful of people who knows the difference between himself and Will.***

*The fact is that no one outside of a handful of people knows the difference between the charlatans, posers and average minds in this space and the scientists like Dominic who are coming up with original work and breaking new ground. **To keep things real—I'm sure Dominic has his faults—and I'm not trying to say nice things just to get this business.** But I believe this is an asset that needs to be used in this crazy Wild West environment where big personalities and big ideas are grabbing the headlines, regardless of whether they are worthy.*

Was I trying to be this guy's best pal or PR consultant? Telling someone you barely know that they are a transcendent genius and then telling them they "have their faults" was not normal communication for engineers—or anyone, really. I didn't hear from them at all, which pissed me off. I followed up about six weeks later, and they said they were still considering their options. I never heard from them again. Dfinity would go on to raise $190 million in private equity over the next year.

Flip Side always seemed to rise up and slap me in the face whenever I was supposed to show my competence. I had to wonder if this problem would somehow magically disappear. I talked to Eileen, and we decided to put our mega-firm on hold. We'd keep it small but hopefully lucrative and only take on as much work as the two of us could handle.

Despite my uneven business-development track record, there was no lack of other prospective clients.

A new phenomenon had sprung up, and it had crypto by the throat: Initial Coin Offerings (ICOs). ICOs, like Initial Public Offerings (IPOs) for traditional stocks, are mechanisms for funding new projects. Anyone with ETH or bitcoin could contribute to the development of a project and, in return, receive ownership in the form of tokens, which could be bought and sold like any other crypto asset.

It was a gold rush. Ethereum competitor Tezos raised $232 million in two weeks. Another competitor, EOS, started a year-long ICO that would eventually raise $4 billion. Yes, billion. Status, an open-source messaging platform and mobile browser for dApps on the Ethereum network, raised $100 million in less than twenty-four hours. Aragon, an Ethereum-based toolset for creating and maintaining decentralized organizations on the Ethereum blockchain, raised $25 million in twenty-six minutes.

The funding for projects like these at the early stages of development would be considered seed rounds in traditional venture funding. Seed rounds usually raise between $50,000 and $2 million. These ICOs suddenly had more money than they would ever need at the earliest stage of their development, before it was clear that their projects were even technically feasible.

We started receiving dozens of requests per week from people wanting PR help for their ICOs. Some of these were get-rich-quick schemes backed by nothing more than a white paper and a pitch. Others were of unknown or questionable provenance. Still others were potentially credible but would require immense, groundbreaking software engineering and blockchain development before coming to fruition.

Alleged scammer LandCoin sent a note with grammatical errors and addressed it to another firm—a cut-and-paste job gone wrong in their frantic effort to blast out the details of their token sale.

Bitconnect is the notorious alleged Ponzi scheme which became a cautionary crypto meme and is the subject of an FBI investigation. They asked if we'd like to advertise on their website.

LevelNet eventually shut itself down after regulators in Vermont took action against them for allegedly making unrealistic claims to investors.

Arthereium was planning an ICO for art collectors. They said cryptocurrency would democratize access to fine art by utilizing blockchain technology, artificial intelligence, and virtual reality.

Paragon, which was founded by a Russian multi-millionaire tech mogul and his wife, a former Miss Iowa, was launching a token for cannabis. The rapper The Game was on their advisory board.

Skedaddle was planning an ICO to launch "Uber for buses."

Fishweight.net created an app "by fisherman for fisherman," which would track the size and weight of the fish they catch.

Heads Up 7 ("By Millennials—For Millennials" … strike one) wanted to create "a live-streaming platform where everybody can make money."

A service that shamelessly stated they grab expired domains, called dropcatching, wanted to pump it up with some ICO money. They concluded their note by stating, "I hope this will seduce you."

Agents on behalf of the descendants of Nikola Tesla wanted our help for a project involving hydroelectricity.

Pomegranate Value Chain needed ICO funds to create a channel to connect pomegranate farmers and pomegranate buyers.

And among the least promising was a note from a gentleman who, through cursory research, turned out to be a freelance writer with many complaints for not completing his projects and not refunding fees. He directed us to lay out our ICO launch strategy in detail, soup to nuts, and he'd get back to us.

It is not my intention to denigrate every project that pitched us. Some of their goals were noble, and I can imagine blockchain solving some of the problems they identified. But it was next to impossible to pick the winners from the losers, the honorable from the crooked. We also received pitches from undeniably legit and promising projects and firms like Sia Coin, Medici Ventures and Airswap.

In one sense, it felt great that there was suddenly so much energy in crypto. But it was unnerving. Every naive overachiever, criminal, and legitimate entrepreneur was trying to squeeze through the narrow ICO passage and raise millions of dollars before this mania ended. The SEC and other regulators around the world, while expressing caution, hadn't fully wrapped their arms around what was happening. ICOs at this time were still in a glorious gray zone. And so the founders of these projects crushed each other and all of us with their emails, Reddit posts, tweets, YouTube videos, and meetups, all intended to shill their particular coin before the gray zone turned red.

And it wasn't just the crypto ICO charlatans who made all the money. The whole thing was like the U.S. stock market before regulation. The book *Patriarch* tells the story of how Joe Kennedy (and scores of others) made their money in the 1920s—not through bootlegging but through insider information. Back then, before the creation of the Securities and Exchange Commission (SEC), getting tips from friends and sweetheart deals from business partners was legal.

The same thing was happening with ICOs. Crypto heavy hitters, with names that would cause a bull run on the token simply by association, were given huge swaths of tokens for free or at severely discounted rates in exchange for their endorsement. Since crypto is fully liquid at all times, those advisers and the ICO leaders themselves were able to cash out and leave all of the unsuspecting noobs with full bags of a coin that would soon crash in value. It was like shooting fish in a barrel.

Later, when it became clear what had been going on, crypto wise man Ryan Selkis called a spade a spade. Ryan is a man I respect for his clear-headed approach to crypto investing. He was an early employee of the Digital Currency Group who led *Coindesk* for two years. He is currently leading a much-needed project called Mesari, which is bringing objective analysis to coin economics and casting light as a disinfectant. He tweeted, *The worst part about the ICO cool down/maturation/whatever you call it: You know a bunch of people who knew better are going to make $$$, leave people holding the bag, never get in trouble, and write in their memoirs they regretted the excesses. Fuck that. Call it out now.*

At the time, few did. Those sweet gains were all anyone seemed to care about. The ICO madness in the spring and summer of 2017 was eclipsing the Ethereum story. ICOs were good for the ETH token in the short term because ICOs could only be purchased with ETH or bitcoin. But it was bad from a brand perspective, and it also complicated the narrative to mainstream investors and enthusiasts. The story in February 2017 was, "Ethereum is transformational technology." Now it was, "If you aren't playing roulette with these crazy crypto ICOs, you're leaving money on the table!"

There has always been a delicate balance between greed and idealism in crypto, a dynamic I could appreciate because it was present in my own mind. When they work together, the result is technology development at breakneck speed. The onslaught of ICOs in 2017 was proof that greed was in control for the foreseeable future. I never invested in a single one, nor did I assist with any PR. I'd like to say I was an idealist, but I was as greedy as the next guy.

I just looked at these projects, even the legit ones, and believed that my best bet, the safest in the insane crypto world, was Ethereum, which seemed to be led by a mature and growing group of developers. My investment in ETH was based on so much research, and I simply didn't have the time or inclination to investigate even more risky propositions. My version of risk was betting a large amount on one coin rather than throwing smaller amounts at a bunch of new projects.

I also couldn't deny the upside and what it portended for the future of blockchain in general and Ethereum in particular. ICOs were the first mainstream embrace of the democratization of funding.

American angel investors and venture capitalists are required to be accredited before investing in the hot tech companies that have made them so rich. Most other first world countries have similar regulations. Accredited investors in the U.S. must have at least one million dollars in liquid wealth. The purpose of the regulation is to protect people from losing everything on speculative investments. But one of the unintended or intended consequences of the law is that accredited investors get access to all the best investment opportunities.

The Ethereum crowdsale in October 2014 was one of the first major open-funding opportunities in crypto. The sale generated the equivalent of $2.3 million. It was a rare opportunity for Joe Public to invest in something early, without being an accredited investor.

While the rules needed to be sorted out and some industry-led or even government-assisted regulations needed to be put in place, the long-game optimist in me was excited. The public could participate in these liquidity events from wherever they were without having to be an accredited investor.

Since most of these ICO tokens would be built on top of the Ethereum blockchain, it was clear that Ethereum had become the go-to for fundraising and innovation. It could host any ambitious decentralization project. While many, maybe most, of these projects would likely go bust, I was confident the cream would rise to the top, and their success would validate their own project's objective and contribute to the overall Ethereum ecosystem.

CHAPTER TWENTY-THREE

BE CAREFUL WHAT YOU ASK FOR

The rise of ETH was so violent and unapologetic, it was unsettling. On May 4, 2017, ETH crossed $84. We were up $2 million.

By this time, Kathleen had made a big investment. She went beyond me by also investing in Ethereum-related ICOs—and she was making a killing. She'd learned a lot about crypto and started taking leadership roles on various projects, managing a Slack for one of them. She was a sixty-year-old public school administrator. No one knew Kathleen's demographic. And it didn't matter, because she was obviously a badass.

Kathleen had always been a gunslinger. We had always shared an affinity for unhealthy addictions and recovery from them, and now we shared this. At family parties, we'd cordon ourselves in a corner of the backyard and compare notes. Not on the tech but about how it felt to be riding this train. Was this supposed to happen to us? When would it stop? What happened if it kept going up? It sounded ridiculous, but we were scared and euphoric at the same time.

While ETH was rising steadily, on any given day, the price could drop 20 percent in a matter of minutes. That's the nature of volatile markets, and ETH was the most volatile market on the planet. One day, the value of our ETH dropped $500,000 during the two-hour period when I was watching a movie in a theater and thankfully had my phone turned off.

At those moments, with so much at stake, I had the gnawing sense that this was too good to be true and that I'd curse myself for the rest of my life for not selling earlier. Trolls would post the suicide prevention hotline on r/EthTrader, and some people who were in too deep or unmoored emotionally used it. One of my favorite personalities on the thread was Lagojesus. He had absurdist humor and the best satire posts, hands-down. One day he posted a sad, cautionary tale about how he would have been rich if he hadn't been greedy and foolish with his coins, eventually trading most of them away during FUD and FOMO cycles.

On the way back from Hawaii, the next trip on our negotiated travel list, I started having trouble breathing. I thought it must be because of the smoking I'd been doing while watching the charts. But the next day, I was still struggling. So I went to my doctor. He thought I might have a blood clot from my flight, which led to an emergency room visit, multiple tests, a big hospital bill and the diagnosis that I was experiencing severe anxiety. Was anything making me anxious?

As Sonny said in *The Godfather*, the world was realizing there was a lot of money in that powder.

Crypto culture was changing like Haight-Ashbury did after the Summer of Love. Like everything in crypto, the change was happening at an unprecedented, breakneck pace, over a period of months rather than years. There was suddenly less interest in changing the world and more interest in acquiring crypto by any means necessary, legal or not.

I was having lunch on Burlingame Avenue one day that spring when I received an email from a family friend. He was a nice older man who was interested in finance. I'd just seen him at a party, and we'd discussed crypto, IRA strategy, and other investment stuff. He attached a Dropbox file that said, *Per our conversation.* It was just like him to send me a file after we talked. But you can never be too careful, so I sent him this note:

Hi Carlo, Can you let me know what this is before I download it? Sometimes viruses masquerade as Dropbox files.

He immediately wrote back:

Lol, It's all about financial plan. I find it very interesting that is why am sharing with you.

With that taken care of, I clicked on the file, thinking it might be the perfect thing to read during lunch. Nothing happened. I clicked on it again. Nothing. Then I took another look at the email and noticed the typos.

"MOTHERFUCKER!" I screamed, to the shock of the lady and her preschooler at the next table. I'd been emailing with the hackers! Had I been targeted? My blog about buying ETH had been read by more than twenty thousand people by this time, so I had to assume it was a possibility. Reasonably, I knew that even though I'd downloaded a virus, hackers would have a hard time getting my crypto. I'd put precautions in place, but really, who the fuck knew what type of new exploit they'd come up with?

I'd heard many stories of crypto folks, savvier than me, who'd had their coins stolen by hackers, including a well-known Asian venture capitalist who'd had his phone ported to a new line, allowing the hackers to bypass his two-factor authentication. This would later surface as a scourge. Many high-profile crypto investors would suffer sophisticated hacks through phone porting, including Michael Terpin, an early crypto pioneer who lost $223 million to hackers and subsequently sued his carrier.

I popped a twenty-dollar bill on the table like the guy in the movies who never cares about getting change. I jumped into my minivan and flew down El Camino to the Apple Store. I waited for my turn, staring out the window at the Build-A-Bear store next door. That was about the least cypherpunk way to handle a hack—waiting in line at the Genius Bar.

Several hours later, I felt as good as I could that whatever I'd been infected with hadn't worked. I told Carlo he'd been hacked, and he said he knew! He just didn't know what to do about it. I recommended he let people know next time. (You stupid old bastard—just kidding, love you, Carlo.)

Amidst it all, ETH kept going up. On May 19, it passed $100. We were up $2.3 million.

As you can imagine, the mainstream press had taken notice. *The New York Times, Forbes, Fortune, The Wall Street Journal* and dozens of other publications devoted long articles to Ethereum, the rise of the ETH token, and the decentralized economy it intended to create.

We were up so much money that it interfered with my mental makeup.

I'd seen the clickbait headlines over the years about people with a condition that caused them to have orgasms at random times, like when they were in a meeting, waiting in line at the grocery store or parking their car. I now knew what that felt like. When I checked my phone I'd often be up another six figures since the last time I looked. I couldn't resist stopping whatever I was doing to pump my fist and shout, "YEESSSS!"

I was taking the dog on longer walks, sleeping less, talking faster, listening to more Nirvana and AC/DC, marinating in my own greatness.

When ETH dipped a few dollars, the orgasms went away, and I had brutal withdrawals. I knew we were still way up. But the short-term price was its own narcotic, sloshing dopamine and serotonin around my brain. When ETH stopped going up or had a mild dip, I'd get snappy with Eileen and the kids.

I was having trouble with my existing clients. BitGo needed a series of data sheets and other materials leading up to Consensus, and it was my job to get them done. The content was difficult and complicated. I'd have to go through a few different people to get the edits I needed.

Then I was approached by one of the best projects in the space, Protocol Labs, which was building a file-sharing service on top of Ethereum to eventually function as a decentralized alternative to the likes of Amazon. Naval Ravikant, one of my heroes, was an investor. Juan Perez, the leader of Protocol Labs, was a personal friend of Vitalik. Now I was talking to him on the phone. He asked if I would write a sample press release so they could see me in action before choosing to bring me onto the project. Normally I'd say, "Of course," and get to work. But I hesitated big time and then eventually, grudgingly, agreed to do it, saying, "I wouldn't normally do this." That wasn't the enthusiasm he was looking for. The truth was I couldn't have cared less.

Whatever he was going to pay me, it wouldn't be worth it. Previously large sums of money were suddenly insignificant. My holy grail, a $10,000 per month contract for PR services, now seemed like a lot of work for little money. I could make $10,000 in the blink of an eye.

I still looked at LinkedIn to see what people were up to. Career advancement was a sport I'd played so long, I liked checking the box scores. An old friend of mine from Georgetown was hired to head up communications at a big financial services company. Like many of the people I knew at Georgetown who grew up in Connecticut or Manhattan, I associated him with old money. This new job couldn't have paid more than $250,000 a year. That was a lot. In the past, I would have been jealous. But I'd made $250,000 that day. I realized I had more money than a lot of people I'd considered permanently higher up the economic ladder.

I felt a strange new mastery over the whole topic of pursuing money, a game I'd played my whole life. Now, with my ETH investment, it was remarkably easy to get rich. I'd see people reposting corporate gibberish articles their bosses had written on LinkedIn, and I'd feel sorry for them. They were trying to advance to a higher position with a bigger salary by pretending that this or that corporate initiative was truly remarkable. They had to pretend the executive with the humblebrag post was showing "great leadership" and that they themselves gave a shit about the mission of their company. Maybe they meant it, but I never did when I applauded the same crap on social media.

My public relations work had dried up, so I could theoretically focus on BitGo. I still couldn't seem to get started on those data sheets. When I tried, I became violently distracted. To counteract my procrastination, I decided to work out of BitGo's office for a few days. There would be nothing for me to do except finish those data sheets. Except I found myself leaving the office, sitting on a bench on California Street, and watching the price of ETH.

Was my problem that BitGo was a corporation, albeit one working in crypto? Was I resisting this assignment on philosophical grounds? That would be noble, but it wouldn't be the truth. The reason was I no longer needed the money. While BitGo was made up of nice people, it didn't matter to the restless savage called Dan Conway. Without the monetary incentive, without the need to pay my mortgage and put food on the table for my family, I no longer had the motivation to do the work. I resigned, leaving them in the lurch. I still feel bad about that.

I hadn't asked Eileen if it was OK to quit BitGo. Now I had to. She'd never been a bohemian. According to her value system, quitting one's job, in most circumstances, was what losers did. Quitting one's job was a small step away from collecting unemployment and eating brunch at a homeless shelter, something no one in her family had ever done.

She was walking out the door on her way to Starbucks. I joined her. It was the first warm day in weeks, and we were both wearing shorts and flip flops, which made me feel like I was already on vacation.

"Hey, remember how I said I was having a problem with those BitGo data sheets?"

"Oh, yeah, you told me about that." I could tell she was worried I was going to tell her the whole thing again as part of my personal therapy process. Or ask her to do them.

We were waiting for the light to turn red to cross the El Camino, the busy boulevard separating our neighborhood from the commercial district downtown.

"Well, I couldn't really get them done no matter how hard I tried." She turned to look at me. These words seemed so weak, much less convincing than when I practiced them. "It was really brutal," I added when she just kept staring. Even I had to admit a pair of data sheets that needed to be written didn't qualify as "brutal." But it was true that I had struggled very hard to get them done and couldn't do it. It still sounds weak, even at the time of this writing, but also true.

"I ended up telling Mike that I was going to move on."

"What do you mean?" A few feet in front of us a bus raced by at a high rate of speed, momentarily throwing Eileen's hair in her face. But her head didn't move.

"I told him it was time to part ways."

The light turned green, but she didn't budge.

"Excuse me?"

"I quit BitGo. We have enough money to get by for now, so don't worry. We have two million dollars!"

Eileen was still getting used to the idea that crypto was real money. But we hadn't sold yet, so it wasn't, actually.

"You have got to be kidding me." She wasn't scared, nervous, or confused. She was fucking pissed. "You quit? So what are you going to do now? I have a ton of client work, and you quit your one client?"

"You can quit, too. We can see how it goes for six months, then go back if we need to."

Her mouth opened half way and she gasped.

"You've gone off the deep end again, Dan. What the fuck are you thinking?"

She hadn't acted this way when we made the big initial investment in ETH, a much riskier and potentially cataclysmic action. But work was something she valued. It was something people did. Especially when they had kids and a lot of expenses, like us. The light was now stale yellow, but she crossed anyway, putting her hand up to slow a car that was trying to turn left in front of her. I stood there on the corner and watched her storm away. I knew it was best to just let her go, and she definitely didn't want my company anyway.

I could see why she was mad, but I had a hard time feeling too bad about it, since I'd made us millions of dollars. I'd been running these numbers in my head for so long, I thought the enormity of that windfall would be obvious to her as well. But I had forgotten that she wasn't obsessed like me with financial independence and the Fourth Industrial Revolution that Ethereum would usher into the world, making us bazillionaires.

Thankfully, ETH kept rising. It kept rising all the way to the agreed-upon time for our first sale. I hadn't talked to Sean in a while. I planned to lay low. Then, as I pulled into the school parking lot for family lunch day, my phone buzzed. I picked it up, and there was that chirpy voice I'd learned to love/hate.

"Congratulations! You've hit your sell target."

Thanks, Sean. Damn. On May 19, I relented, and we sold 4,130 ETH at approximately $125 per coin for $513,000. This was the total needed to recover our initial investment and pay the taxes on our gain. We'd unloaded a big chunk of our ETH a week before Consensus 2017 in Times Square on May 22-24, a.k.a. Blockchain Homecoming for nerds like me.

Ultimately, I felt good about this sale. Eileen was still mad at me, which was sobering. Now I knew we at least couldn't lose everything if ETH crashed. I'd still need to go back to work, though. That was an odious proposition that I didn't care to contemplate.

CHAPTER TWENTY-FOUR

HODL ON FOR DEAR LIFE

I was attending Consensus on my own dime. I didn't have any professional networking requirements, so I mainly hung out by myself, monitoring the whole thing and avoiding BitGo people. I was successful other than one uncomfortable escalator interaction with Mike Belshe, who was polite yet exited the escalator quickly enough to suggest he no longer enjoyed my company. The way I left them high and dry, I didn't blame him.

I did see some fellow r/EthTraders and some eccentric crypto YouTube personalities. It was like meeting cartoon characters in the flesh. The context I associated them with was so virtual, I'd forgotten that they existed in real life.

My area of operation made me feel even more like I was in a dream land. Consensus was happening at the Marriott Marquis. Right next door was *Hamilton*, which represented the first purchase we'd made with our new funds and portended a potential new life of not worrying about money. A few buildings over, available by passage through a grungy door that looked more like a hole in the wall, was the 46th Street Recovery House, which was open from 10:30 a.m. to 11:30 p.m. and hosted meetings every hour. I'd have to stay sober, literally and figuratively, if I was going to translate this crypto windfall into something transformative in the real world. With ETH-mania running through me and the recovery support I was getting from the twelve-step meetings I still regularly attended, I hadn't craved drugs or alcohol for a long time. Flip Side was perfectly satisfied for now with being rich and right about ETH.

Consensus was glitzy. It had just the right touch of mainstream energy with crypto-credible content. The Tapscotts were there and said some polished shit, bless their hearts. Some crypto titans had debates on Bitcoin scaling, the never-ending civil war plaguing that community. But Ethereum had the most buzz. In his keynote, Coinbase CEO Brian Armstrong unveiled a new Ethereum-based messaging app called Toshi (later renamed Coinbase Wallet). It was similar to WeChat, a messaging and payment app ubiquitous in China. The popular teen messaging app, Kik, announced they were launching their own token on the Ethereum blockchain.

The Enterprise Ethereum Alliance (EEA) announced eighty-six new members, including Bancor, Deloitte, Mitsubishi, and Broadridge. A *Forbes* article on May 22 by the crypto journalist Laura Shin included what I considered the understatement of the year: "The EEA new members include both financial services incumbents and blockchain startups, and span industries, including state government, health, and entertainment. The diversity of the members in terms of industry and age **suggests the possibility for disruptive innovation.**" (Emphasis mine)

Crypto suddenly wasn't so weird anymore. The old-timers couldn't believe how quickly things had changed. Even Bitcoin veterans who'd been through the explosion of interest in Bitcoin in 2013 were shocked.

ETH's sweet smile kept lighting me up. On a break, I took a cab downtown to the Freedom Tower. As I waited in line, ETH crossed $200. We were up $4.5 million.

Everything that I thought would happen after Consensus occurred, but more so. Over the next few weeks, ETH just exploded upwards. I'm searching for words to get the point across because I've already had to describe how our investment had risen 1,500 percent in three months. That just doesn't happen. But now we went to fairyland, a place where men like me get suited up in leotards and dance around with butterflies in their hair (or lack thereof), spreading love, eating ice cream sundaes, and yes, driving Lambos.

Between the last day of Consensus on May 24 and June 12, I kid you not, ETH doubled again, hitting $400. We were up $9 million. I hadn't yet agreed to our next exit plan with Sean and Eileen. Sean sent me a note, which I ignored. It didn't matter, because I was a god.

Not only was I a god, but with this historic ETH boom, I was also Nostradamus. I'd never exhibited an ability to prognosticate before. Previously, I'd always been trying to catch up to new trends just as they petered out. At Safeway, I had tried to become an expert in healthcare policy too late, just as Obamacare made the real experts highly valuable. In the 1990s, I signed up for swing dance lessons after watching *Swingers*, right before the fad disappeared.

But now, like a character out of the Bible who does something insane because God told him to, I'd ended up being right about ETH. I was right in the middle of one of the most profound disruptions the world would ever see.

It felt like I'd taken a driver out of my bag on a par five and, rather than hitting a shank, I drove it four hundred yards down the middle of the fairway. Every moment during this period, I had the same feeling as watching that shot as it soared farther than anyone thought possible, while my playing partners looked on in admiration. The feeling rang in my hands, head, soul.

I knew I'd reminisce about this time for the rest of my life. The feeling was so different than anything I had ever experienced. I was suddenly the man I always wanted to be—a fucking legend with a huge set of balls.

***

ETH's price was rising at an unprecedented pace over a period of days and weeks rather than the expected months and years. Anecdotally, from comments on r/EthTrader, it seemed like a lot of large investors had a sell target of $400.

People who'd invested in the crowdsale and other whales who'd gotten in under five dollars suddenly had life-changing money. They started running for the doors.

On June 24, ETH took a dive. From an all-time high of $400, it spat up, then puked up its gains. It was like a sick animal that might very well die.

Those selling their ETH disgusted me. For months, I'd seen these same people claiming, "I wish I'd heard about this a year ago. I would have bought a big stash!" Bullshit. Now that ETH was headed back down, their FOMO had turned to FUD. These run-of-the-mill conventional thinkers and cowards were bleeding us dry. Now more than ever, true believers needed to HODL. Anything else would cause a tragedy of the commons, when each individual's supposedly rational action leads directly to total destruction for everyone, including them.

By June 27, it was at $272, a forty percent decrease in five days. Sean sent me an email.

ETH may go below $200 for a year or longer. I'm only saying this so that you and Eileen can make the best decision

When I didn't respond, he sent me another email asking if we could get together for a walk to tell each other about our recent family vacations. Nice try. I blew him off. I didn't care to spend time with Chicken Littles. I wasn't going to sell.

Then it all came tumbling down.

CNBC blared, "Ethereum is crashing by 20 percent right now after confidence in Bitcoin rival shaken."

Of course, there was no new reason why confidence would be shaken other than the drop in price, but that didn't matter. And it was actually crashing 20 percent every few days.

On July 11, 2017, ETH declined to $211.

The glory of being a whale had turned into a nightmare. We were losing hundreds of thousands of dollars every time I checked the price. More than a million dollars a week. We were down five million from our all-time high. We'd only taken out our original investment.

***

On July 2, we started our second fabulous agreed-to family vacation, a seven-day trip to Cinque Terre on the Italian Riviera. Eileen and I had honeymooned there fourteen years before. We both loved the cold Mediterranean water, gelato, and hikes through each of those five ancient villages which were connected by mountain trails.

I hoped the rustic setting and spotty Internet would allow me to unplug. I also knew that pulling a "geographic," a well-known concept in recovery circles, wouldn't save me from the demons I was running from in the crypto markets. As they say, "Wherever you go, there you are." I knew this bear market could get much uglier, no matter where I was.

We checked into our private apartment in the middle of our home-base village, Riomaggiore. Our neighborhood was lovely and filled with people selling flowers and focaccia, good-looking Italians drinking espresso in impossibly small cups, and herds of overweight American couples bickering as they trudged up the steep hill to the train station. I painted a smile on my face and took it all in.

As we prepared to go to the beach, it was time to slather suntan lotion on the kids. We'd be out in the sun all day, so I wanted them to have a good base layer. It'd be hard to corral them later. Annie was first, and she was the one who hated it the most. She was ten years old and very focused on her appearance.

Now I blocked out her complaints as I started in. The sun was bright, but I'd probably remember this as a dark period of my life, I thought. I flashed back to when I first bought crypto and agreed to these trips. I was trying to remember what that felt like. Suddenly, I was interrupted by a scene right in front of me, literally in the palms of my hands. Annie had looked in the mirror and was shrieking like she'd seen a ghost. Her face was completely white, as if she'd been painted with a brush. Eileen looked over and said, "Oh no," and covered her mouth. Annie believed I had permanently disfigured her.

I started crying myself because I was laughing so hard. "I'm sorry, Annie, I was daydreaming! Don't worry, we'll take care of it."

Eileen cleaned her up, but a weight had lifted. I was brought back to the present. The terror of our volatile investment was still with me, but I could hold it at bay for a few more days.

I was proud of myself. Halfway into the trip, and I still hadn't checked the price. But on our fourth morning, I was in a cafe next door, waiting for everyone else to wake up. They had WiFi. So I looked. And we were down another $500,000.

When crypto crashes, no one has any idea when or if it will stop dropping. It doesn't matter what we had on paper because it was all falling through our fingers. Crypto can rise like a bottle rocket or tank like an ocean liner. The price moves way past what is considered polite. And when it was falling before my eyes in June and July 2017, with still-low liquidity, it would have been difficult to get out even if I had wanted to without causing a bigger bloodbath in the market. Selling on the way down, as I had attempted to do a year earlier after the DAO fiasco, was the trap that every bear wanted you to step in. It was out of the question.

As I sat in a cafe, looking out over the Mediterranean and getting ready to gobble up some delicious, salty focaccia, I felt like a defiant don of the Old World. I didn't care if it was the smart thing to do. I wasn't going to sell on a drop. This wasn't an investment. It was a belief system, a lifestyle.

***

We met a nice Italian couple. They owned a restaurant that we went to almost daily. Ennio hosted, and Martina waited tables. He told us how he had lived in America years before, then made the decision to come back to open his own cafe.

We said Cinque Terre was a great place. He shrugged and said it was just ok, that it was hard to get ahead here. He said that back in America, he'd been able to do the same thing and make a lot more money.

We met them at the beach on our last day. They looked fashionable as hell, of course. But there was a sadness in Ennio's eyes that apparently involved money. I wondered if money would solve his problems.

During this period, I always found an opening to talk about crypto with the people we met. While everyone else was swimming, Ennio and I sipped San Pellegrinos. He told me that the 2008 great recession had screwed them. This was clearly my opening, but I didn't say a word. I didn't have the heart to even imply that we had a lot of money, considering his situation. I also hadn't checked the price for several days. I didn't know if we were still among the fortunate.

That night, as everyone else was sleeping, I stayed awake and let myself think through what we'd experienced. I hoped to God (who certainly had more important matters to deal with) that I wouldn't end up like Ennio, neutered and defeated due to lack of funds. I couldn't deny that we would have had millions in our pockets if we had sold earlier.

It's hard selling into a big rise. Following Consensus in May 2017, when ETH was spiraling up, talk on r/EthTrader was that ETH would hit $2,000 or higher in the coming months. Even at that high price, the entire Ethereum blockchain, with hundreds of dApps still in production and preparing to be sprung on the world in the coming years, wouldn't be valued as much as Facebook, Amazon, or Apple. For a technology that might very well be the next World Wide Web, it seemed to me it could, and should, go a lot higher.

I continued thinking about these things during my least favorite part of our Italy trip, driving out of Cinque Terre on a mountain road designed to generate the headline, *American Family Smashed on Rocks, Father's Head Found Floating in Ocean.* We'd gotten to know our driver on the long drive from Milan to the Riviera a week before. He was macho and friendly and generous. He'd warned us that Sicily was too dangerous to visit, but he wasn't as concerned about driving safely. I asked if these roads freaked him out, a question that any sane person would answer with, "Yeah!" But he didn't take the hint. He accelerated. I realized his own self-worth was tied up in navigating these roads at a high rate of speed, damn the consequences.

I was aware that approaching the Italian psyche in a ham-fisted way could be dangerous. I might make a cultural blunder and profoundly insult him. But I could see our lives flashing before my eyes on each turn as we peered over the abyss. I was already at my capacity for tolerating danger.

Matteo started humming. I peered over a jagged cliff and saw nothing but sky and ocean. "Matteo! I'm sorry, but for my sake, can you please slow down?"

He did, but the car fell silent for the rest of the ride to Milan, where we spent our final night in a swanky hotel before flying home the next morning.

***

As we prepared to reenter the real world with its ubiquitous Internet connections, I thought of our exit points and asked myself if I should have sold earlier. The timing of when to buy and sell crypto is an excruciating decision. My trouble illustrates the obvious difficulties of selling at the right time, but the buy and hold decision is just as daunting. Sometimes a person's enthusiasm for a decentralized world isn't wed to a conviction to invest (or gamble, depending on your perspective).

Thanks to my experience with technologies that went viral, determination to get out of the rat race, addictive personality, ability to handle risk, plus the availability of funds at just the right time and a wife who let me spend them, I was destined to go big once I got the crypto bug. Many others, including a good number of crypto veterans, had not done so, even though they'd been a part of the movement way before me, when bitcoin and ETH prices were dirt cheap and it was possible to pick up a thousand bitcoin for a thousand dollars.

One person in this boat was particularly shocking. In late 2017, Bitcoin evangelist and icon Andreas Antonopoulos announced that he was struggling financially. It was inconceivable to me that he hadn't bought and held bitcoin when it was under twenty dollars. I had assumed he had the equivalent of at least twenty to thirty million by this time, considering how early he was to the game. He was one of the smartest people in crypto, a genius at communicating the enormity of Satoshi Nakamoto's invention and what it meant for society. He flew all over the globe, spreading the word.

But he wasn't able to hold a stash due to other financial pressures, even though only a few thousand dollars invested and held at those low prices would have been worth at least a million dollars a few years later. He had been left out of the get-rich-quick part of the revolution he helped to create. He was way over on the polar opposite side from the ICO charlatans on the greed/idealist spectrum. For that, I respected him immensely, although I shuddered to think of being in his shoes. Eventually, he ended up raising approximately one hundred bitcoins from crypto millionaires.

On a smaller scale, I recognized this strange caution from friends in my life. They'd get excited about the possibility of gains, then hem and haw about investing a thousand dollars. Seriously? These people would never have had the guts to find a drug dealer. For better or worse, I was just built differently. While I'd never be a professional leader of the movement, you could count on me to go on a suicide mission like some drunken patriot on behalf of my own glory and Vitalik Buterin. I loved that man, but I hoped I wasn't on one right now.

I checked my phone at the airport. ETH had fallen another 20 percent. We'd lost an additional $1.2 million since the start of our trip.

***

Even amidst the crash, the stupid ICOs kept coming, wanting our help. In total, we received more than a hundred requests from projects all over the globe, sometimes in broken English or what appeared to be Russian or Mandarin. They were causing too much confusion in the market. I'd already stopped answering new business emails and changed my LinkedIn profile to show Zealot was no longer active. But they still found us. So I shut down the Zealot Communications website entirely, hoping they'd leave us alone.

My low point came one day in mid-July when I was helping my aunt clean out her apartment. Some other relatives were also helping, and they kept asking me about ETH. Between the realization that we'd be digging through dusty boxes for the next few hours and that my ETH-based freedom might be gone forever, I felt ill and had to rest outside the room for a few minutes.

On July 16, 2017, ETH sank to $133. We were still up $3 million. But it was dropping, and I kept thinking of how I didn't have any clients and how I'd burned a bridge with BitGo.

More than anything, I was pissed. That night I logged into r/EthTrader and pounded out this defiant screed to rally the troops:

I won't sell a single damn coin during this downturn. I'll let it go to zero before capitulating. I didn't get into Ethereum as a normal investor, I got into this as a true believer, and that is what I am today. (Yes, I'm a verified moonkid, trolls—check back with me in a few months and a few years, and let's compare notes.).

Ethereum grabbed a hold of me in a way that no other technology ever has. Its potential inspired me. I could feel it in my bones, and I still do. So I don't treat my investment in ETH as a stock or a mutual fund—I treat it as a bet on a better future, on something big that requires vision and balls in order to stay the course.

When this thing turns back up ... hold on tight, because you are going to see something truly extraordinary. Or you can try to time the market, sell now and panic buy as the exchanges shut down and you are stuck with fiat.

But I'm ready to sacrifice all of my dear profits all the way down to the bottom, because like Kaiser Soze, I'd rather kill my dear coins entirely than give up hope and sell into this Fear, Uncertainty and Doubt.

Kaiser Soze killed his wife and children rather than give his enemies leverage. Looking back, that's a pretty serious comparison. I knew that by holding I was risking the substantial windfall we'd already won. But my goal was fuck-you money. Period. I had no interest in getting a nice nest egg and then going back to work. I wanted out of the workforce. I'd already left. I wasn't going back.

Eileen was still not asking about the price, so I didn't bring it up.

***

Even amidst the drop, people from all over the world wanted in. The devastation I was living was a buying opportunity for many. By this time, the crypto infrastructure was creaking under the weight of increased activity. All of the buying and now all of the selling was slowing down the exchanges, making it hard for people to get money in or out. Coinbase reported that they were signing up fifty thousand new customers *per day* in 2017.

God help you if you needed technical support. It simply wasn't available. If your application or trading was irregular in any way, the exchanges would simply freeze your account rather than risk running afoul of the Know Your Customer (KYC) and Anti-Money Laundering (AML) guidelines they were trying to follow. They simply didn't have enough staff to fix individual problems. They were in full triage mode, which left thousands of customers at the biggest exchanges, especially Coinbase, with no recourse. Three of my friends simply couldn't get their applications approved and moved to second-tier exchanges with more difficult fiat on-ramps and sketchier provenance.

It seemed that everyone I'd ever told about crypto wanted to talk with me. The guy at the mailbox store where I made copies, the nice motherly lady at my Saturday night twelve-step meeting, an old colleague from Acme who had been cast off like me, old friends of Eileen who had seen my crypto posts on Facebook, my own college and high school friends, and even the neighbor down the street who was a retired insurance salesman.

Did I know of another exchange that could sign them up quick? Should they sell their ETH? They've sold their ETH. Should they buy back in? Is bitcoin going to pop? What's the next big ICO? Is this crash a buying opportunity? Excitement and mania and panic and FOMO and FUD all danced together around a campfire as I slowly turned on the spit, my dream of a clean exit cooked right out of me.

I told all of the people contacting me that I wasn't talking about crypto right now. As the voicemails, emails, and tagged Facebook posts piled up, I wanted to leave an auto reply that said: *JUST HOLD ETH, YOU FUCKING COWARDS.*

CHAPTER TWENTY-FIVE

HEAD ABOVE WATER

During this troubling time, I did what I always did when my hands were shaking. I visited r/Ethereum, where the discussion is focused on product development, not the price of ETH. Before raw price movements took over my brain, this was where I had spent a lot of time trying to scratch out what was happening. I'd collect signals from third parties building things on Ethereum. I'd evaluate the logic of developers who said this or that could be disrupted at future stages. Not quite quantitative analysis, but it's what I was capable of.

The dialogue and collaboration in the Ethereum developer community never stopped, no matter what was happening, price-wise. The Metropolis Part 1 upgrade, named Byzantium, was being finalized. It would make the Ethereum Virtual Machine more approachable and provide smart contract developers more options and stability. zk-SNARKS functionality was also being prepared, which would soon add the most advanced privacy features to the Ethereum blockchain. At a technical level, I knew enough about these things to grunt, "Good," before flipping back to r/EthTrader to see if the price had stopped dropping.

I always knew Ethereum was raw, experimental in most ways, and fraught with difficult development hurdles in the months and years ahead, especially the challenge to scale while remaining decentralized—the blockchain holy grail. But visiting r/Ethereum now gave me confidence. The rational side of my investor brain, the side that had never been drawn to a speculative investment before ETH, was still satisfied with the empirical evidence. It still seemed that Ethereum had no bounds, that time and development hours were the only critical barriers to achieving widespread adoption, one decentralized app at a time.

***

ETH had more to say, despite the ICO madness and the glee of skeptics during the summer crash.

In early August, it started going back up, and fast. On August 8, it hit $275. I saw Sean at a drop-off for one of our sons' mutual friend's birthday party. I looked him in the eye and asked, "When are you going to tell me about that family vacation?"

I was ready for our next cash-out. A sum my previous self would have considered a massive, unbelievable, piss-my-pants-in-jubilation amount of money.

Why now? This was the best way to ensure that I could still hold an enormous stack no matter what crypto had in store for us. Cashing out a large chunk also allowed me to make a deal with Eileen that would remove additional pressure. With this money, we could live for years without working. This gave her the confidence to join me in the world of Not Having a Job, at least for the time being. This was good news, because she was growing tired of meeting client deadlines while I tinkered with the initial outline of this book at Philz Coffee and complained about what hard work it was.

I agreed that if she quit her remaining clients, and then everything went to shit and ETH collapsed, I'd be the one having to go back to work first. I was extremely confident, rightly or wrongly, that with a multi-year runway, ETH would rise up in value, making my miserable return to work theoretical only.

On August 31, we sold 7,365 ETH at approximately $366 for $2.7 million, leaving us with about two million after tax. I wired it to Wells Fargo, lickety-split, no problems at all. I could see the money right there. Two-point-seven million. U.S. dollars. In our account. The vases didn't fall off the wall, my eyes didn't bleed, paparazzi didn't gather on the front lawn. But we now had two million, after tax, sitting in our bank account. Ho-hum.

Eileen didn't seem to register the two million the same way I did. She was happy, of course, but ready to move on after a brief conversation. I could spend all day talking about the money we now had, the big money we might still get. Her instinct was that these conversations were unholy, so she avoided them.

Despite her reticence, we also discussed the elephant in the room—our plan to eventually sell the majority of our coins to earn permanent financial independence. This had been the goal all along, and it suddenly seemed plausible. Sean ran the numbers. We would unquestionably be set for life with nine million dollars, after taxes. We could live a fabulous life, spending the interest and principal as necessary. We could weather any financial crisis. That was now the goal. But while we agreed on the total dollar amount we needed, we didn't settle on a final number of ETH we would keep. I had no intention of selling all of our ETH, no matter how high it went in the short term. So we didn't have a firm sell strategy.

In the fall of 2017, we were in a benign purgatory. We had no income, but we had plenty of money. It was suspended animation. It felt like the cord could be cut at any moment, even though our bank account said otherwise. I was still totally aligned with Flip Side. We were celebrating our vision and guts. But in the back of my mind, I thought of the Kennedys. I often wondered if they'd brought down mythical forces upon them for reaching so high. Now I couldn't shake the thought that maybe I'd done the same.

My sister, who'd already raised her four children and needed less money than us, made her move. On October 1, 2017, she completed selling two million dollars worth of ETH and retired permanently. At her going-away party, everyone wanted to know about this mysterious investment that had skyrocketed. Was it too late to get in? It always is, isn't it?

On October 9, 2017, on the eve of Kathleen's trip of a lifetime to India, the Tubbs Fire descended on Santa Rosa like a blowtorch and burned her house to the ground. The fire was so fierce and caused such devastation that it led the national news for days. The next morning, after staying up all night watching coverage, I noticed my thumb was trembling. A quick Google search confirmed my suspicion. This could be the first sign of ALS. Was the universe balancing out our good fortune?

On November 15, I was eating lunch with my mom, sister, and brother, when I received a text from Eileen. "Were you trying to add a phone to our account?" She'd received a text from our carrier. This sounded like phone porting, the most devastating crypto theft exploit. I jumped up as if something had sunk its fangs into me, startling my mother and hitting my head on the umbrella at this suddenly annoying sidewalk bistro. I stormed down the street, yelling into my phone at Eileen like I was trying to sell a thousand shares of stock before the market crashed in *Trading Places*.

"Can you please CALL THEM NOW?" I pleaded.

She was at yard duty at the school and wasn't allowed to make a call. I let my voice go low and said, "It needs to be you who calls, because you received the text. If you want to see it all get stolen, that's fine."

She exited the yard and made the call. It turned out to be a phony text, a phishing attempt by hackers impersonating our carrier. As long as Eileen hadn't clicked on the link (she hadn't), we were fine. Thankfully no child was injured during her absence from yard duty, as far as I know. At least my thumb had stopped trembling.

Eileen wasn't thrilled with my reaction. I apologized. I realized we needed help on the cybersecurity front. So we splurged on a private digital security firm that now monitors every Internet-connected device in our family and employs other security measures. We also installed a home alarm system. I considered getting a weapon but realized I was going overboard.

***

Through October and November, ETH hibernated, holding its price for what seemed like a year. In crypto, this was usually a sign that something batshit crazy was about to happen.

In Taipei, on November 25, Vitalik gave a detailed lecture about the future of Ethereum. He laid out the road map for what he dubbed Ethereum 2.0 and explained how Ethereum would implement a theoretical scalability breakthrough called sharding and a new smart contract programming language called Viper. He also spoke at length about the eventual upgrade from Ethereum's proof of work algorithm, which most blockchains, including Bitcoin, utilized. Ethereum was moving to proof of stake, which would allow exponentially faster transactions. It would enable real decentralized apps for the first time.

ETH started climbing again, this time with determination. After sitting below $400 for the previous few months, it quickly rose to $475.

And then it became clear that the fall break was just the eye of the storm as ETH picked up its Category 5 fury. Everything jumped back into action.

The crypto and business press were eager to be the first to announce the next ETH bull. *Seeking Alpha* blared, "Buy Ethereum Now, Before Its Tech Takes Off."

It was furious. It was crazy. It was a once-in-a-lifetime storm surge, and we just needed to hold on. On December 12, 2017, ETH hit $522. We were up $8 million on our remaining ETH.

This is fucking nuts, agreed everyone everywhere.

On December 14, 2017, ETH hit $700. We were making more than a million dollars a day. We were up $10 million on our remaining ETH.

Once again, I couldn't get over how right I'd been. I would sit on the same couch where I'd had my humiliating video interview eleven months before and relive what was happening to us, even though I was still living it. I'd been in this fever dream for a while. It was like one day I had claimed aliens were going to land in our backyard. Everyone thought I was crazy. Then, one day, the most powerful spotlight anyone had ever seen shone down on our house. Our dog started barking, the kids panicked and Eileen ran to get the suitcases. "They've arrived!" I'd say. "Nothing to worry about—they are friendly."

Vitalik, the oldest soul in the room, someone who never seemed to care much about the price of ETH, chimed in on Twitter about the growing discrepancy between the price of ETH and its promising yet still immature technology:

> *How many unbanked people have we banked? How much censorship-resistant commerce for the common people have we enabled? How many dApps [distributed applications] have we created that have substantial usage? How much value is stored in smart contracts that actually do anything interesting? How many Venezuelans have actually been protected by us from hyperinflation? How much actual usage of micropayment channels is there actually in reality?*

Interesting questions, but none of us cared, because we were making so much money.

Now everyone in the world wanted to know about crypto. The interest level felt ten times more intense than it had been just a few months earlier. My twelve-year-old son Danny told me he wanted to buy Komodo coin. It's a sure thing, he said. He also told me he was going to start his own blog called The Crypto Kid. What the hell did he know about it?

I flipped on the show *Silicon Valley* to get my mind off everything, only to realize the entire Season Four was based on a technology that sounded a lot like Ethereum. I turned it off when Pied Piper suffered a 51 percent attack, a crypto doomsday scenario involving a blockchain being destroyed.

Of course, I was having trouble sleeping. I'd wake up at three a.m. and feel those scratchy sheets in the downstairs guest bedroom where I sometimes slept when I was restless and didn't want to wake Eileen. I refused to check the price of ETH. But I always did. Then my body got used to the drill, and I'd wake up every night at the witching hour, looking for my fix. This kind of thing wasn't supposed to happen unless you were in a movie or the subject of an urban legend.

Ethereum was in the Tornado, a term coined by Geoffrey Moore and well-known in tech circles, when everyone wants a piece of the technology, wants to be a part of it in any way possible. All they had to do was buy ETH.

A new meme called the Flippening took hold in the crypto community and mainstream press. It refers to the moment when Ethereum overtakes Bitcoin as the blockchain with the most value. Both coins had skyrocketed, but ETH was going up more. Were the Flippening to occur, ETH would replace bitcoin as the first crypto among peers. ETH would become the crypto reserve currency with the most fiat on-ramps. Its price would go ballistic.

I always thought ETH would skyrocket when the first dApp achieved mainstream usage a year or two or three down the line. Even to a speculator like me, this felt too much, too fast. But maybe this was what the Beatles felt like when they got too big, too fast. Ultimately, who cared, they were the Beatles!

On December 20, 2017, ETH hit $827. We were up $12 million on our remaining ETH.

Then, of course, Sean called me. He asked if we wanted to meet again now that we could achieve our goal of financial independence. I liked that idea. This would be a victory lap, an opportunity to talk about ETH in a focused way for an hour.

As Eileen and I walked through the door, we were greeted by one of his junior staffers who loved to talk about crypto.

"Wow, crazy times!" he said. "How are you guys doing?"

"Well, I'll tell you, it's really strange and glorious at the same time. ETH is about to overtake Bitcoin, and then the real show will start. It's like the Wild West. Very insane and obviously good for us."

I felt like a celebrity.

Then I told anecdotes about r/EthTrader speculation, crypto hacks, mainstream press coverage, people I knew who were now jumping in to invest and other related stories. I kept talking even as we were sitting down in the boardroom with Sean and the rest of the team waiting for me to finish so we could start the meeting.

I remembered how Prince Charming, at the top of his game at Acme, used to go off on personal anecdotes that he found amusing. He didn't seem to care if others had to listen to them, because what he was saying was obviously worth it. Now I was happy to share my charming observations and tangents with this group.

Finally, the meeting started. Sean had prepared.

An assistant flipped on the overhead projector. Suddenly there were charts and graphs. Each showed different cash-out scenarios for turning our ETH into dollars. Each scenario delivered the same punchline: it was almost time. It just depended on how much ETH I wanted to keep for the long term, how much skin I still wanted in the game.

I'd been running my own numbers in my head, and I was having a hard time tracking my calculations to Sean's. It was confusing. His charts reminded me of prison cells.

"So, you guys are facing a decision. Which of these scenarios lines up with what you want to do?"

I had to figure out how to balance what I thought Eileen might want with my own still-murky exit plan and these perfectly crafted options that Sean had just explained to us for ten minutes.

"Well, we are in a good spot, clearly," I said. "There are just some questions we still need to think about, and we also need to think about what might happen next. I've always wanted to stop working, and so does Eileen…" Blah, blah, blah.

I wasn't making much sense. The contrast between Sean's verbal presentation and my own was extreme. This was like a meeting at Acme. I started to feel a physical aversion to sitting in this room with these people. Sean seemed so in control. He said the right things, his people respected him, he was able to share a joke and then smoothly transition back to the work at hand. I thought of the time at Acme when I told a joke during a critical meeting with a bunch of executives, then forgot to show the final slide of my presentation because I was so caught up in the laughs.

I just wasn't good at this stuff. But now I was sitting in this room because I'd done something Sean would never do. I'd identified something and had the guts to go all in. Flip Side and me were aligned, and it was beautiful. Sean was a fucking bean counter, and I was a bandit, a revolutionary, an icon. We'd made $300,000 between waking up that morning and sitting with him and his perfectly manicured team.

Eileen was hanging on his every word, throwing me sideways glances at any mention of the stakes.

Flip Side had heard enough. He leaned into my ear and said, *"THIS IS AN INTERVENTION. GET THE FUCK OUT OF HERE."*

I interrupted Sean. "Wait a minute, I got here first. I'm not going to give it all up now!"

The room fell silent. Eileen was looking at me, actually leaning in my direction. She said, "But Dan, isn't that the point?"

And like that, I'd been outplayed. The point was to become financially independent and keep a meaningful amount of ETH for the long term. I'd made that clear. As risky a play as that had been, at least it was a measurable goal. And we had basically achieved it. We could walk away right now with financial independence and at least a thousand ETH. But I seemed to be moving the goalposts, and I couldn't or wouldn't articulate why.

"Ok, let's continue, and we will have to think about all of this," I said.

For the rest of the meeting, I kept my cards close to my vest and didn't let myself show enthusiasm or anger. As we were leaving, Sean tried to pivot back to friendly ground.

"I was telling the folks here about that movie we saw. What a trip!"

A few weeks before, Sean and Cathy had joined Eileen and me for a movie that was kind of crappy and also gory in a funny way. But I wasn't willing to go there.

"Yeah, that was a trip," I said.

Eileen picked up the banter, and then we left.

A couple of days later, I was greeting parents who were picking up their kids after a sleepover at our house. One of the moms who knew I was into crypto asked, "What do you think about all of this mania?"

"Well, there is mania, and it's getting pretty extreme. But that's not surprising. Crypto is the first decentralized technology to make it—it's a game changer."

"No, it's not," she said. "Wikipedia is decentralized."

"Nope. Wikipedia is crowdsourced content. It is still run out of centralized services controlled by a few people."

"Listen, Dan, I've been working in tech for a long time, and I can tell you, it's decentralized, and there are others. All of these tech bros getting rich is amazing, though."

I'd heard enough of this bullshit. So many people who'd missed the boat were ready to curse crypto without understanding it. Ethereum was bigger than these people could comprehend. But the fantastical price increase had opened it up for attack. Crypto was suddenly like an overexposed celebrity, and everyone was rooting for it to fail.

I looked her in the eye, without a hint of a smile. "You're dead wrong."

A couple of days later, she posted something on Facebook mocking all of the crypto zealots and complaining about how dealing with them was such a pain in the ass. I almost added a snarky comment but thought better of it. I actually like her. And I'd been an asshole. I should have just laughed it off when she mentioned Wikipedia.

A few weeks later, *The New York Times* published an article, "Everyone is Getting Hilariously Rich, and You're Not." It profiled a host of people who had made millions. They were described as douchebags. The article summed up the philosophy of these people:

"Over long hours in anonymous group chats, San Francisco bars and Settlers of Catan game nights, they talk about how cryptocurrency will decentralize power and wealth, changing the world order."

Amen. They might have been douchebags, I might be a douchebag, but this was worth fighting for, especially since it was making us so hilariously rich.

***

One would expect that Eileen and I would have had a big conversation after the meeting with Sean, before she left for Boston with the kids for their annual Christmas trip. But we didn't, even after I seemed to be unwilling to list an amount of ETH I was determined to hold onto. It's hard to believe, but I've confirmed with her that this was the case. She simply had an amazing ability to compartmentalize the crypto stuff and block it all out, no matter how good or bad the news seemed to be.

CHAPTER TWENTY-SIX

NOW

A few days after Eileen and kids left for Boston, ETH started shaking upwards again in great bursts that temporarily froze the exchanges due to all of the money flowing in. It was like a 9.0 earthquake with an infinite number of 9.0 aftershocks. On January 3, it hit $900. I received an email from Sean.

There's a sudden sea change on crypto. Our clients have been vaguely interested for awhile. Today I took *three* calls from clients, the type of client who generally has little interest in the details of investing, asking about bitcoin. Then we got publicity photos taken (we have a new analyst who started this week) and the photographer told us he's going to stop shooting photos because he's day trading crypto and he's made $2 mil this year. Then I went to a prospect meeting with a pair of 80 year old clients. Their first question? What do you think about bitcoin.

Never before in my career have I seen this level of interest in a rapidly increasing investment. And never has this sort of interest been a good sign.

I'd be derelict as your advisor to not pass this on to you. If these 5 people all turn out to have been right about wanting

*to buy crypto now... I'll be shocked. But in the near term it
can of course keep rocketing higher.*

Oh, shit. That morning I'd gone for a run, and now two hours
later, I was still sitting on the couch in my sweaty clothes. I
hadn't eaten. I hadn't even gotten coffee yet.

These interactions with Sean were starting to feel like the
ominous warning signs before a tsunami. *Hey, the ocean is
receding, what do you think that is all about? Hmmm, I wonder
why that flock of six million crows is flying over our resort toward
the mountains?* I loved movies like that, but it felt bad to be
the lead character and not know if I was saved or dead.

There was movement in my rational brain. It was trying to
wake up, dammit. Flip Side was having none of it. He didn't
want to go back in the closet, especially after all he'd done for
me. He'd taken me this far. *What the fuck was my problem? If
$10 million felt good, how fucking great would $50 million feel?*

I willed myself to pull my computer out of my bag and fire
it up. I told the dog, who had been barking, to *shut the fuck
up.* I was trying to figure out if I could do something that I
didn't really want to do. I was ripping my two personalities
apart. It hurt.

I meant to click onto Gemini to check the price and order-
book. Twenty minutes later, I found myself on r/EthTrader,
high on crypto again. There was a full orgy going on. The
main feed had fourteen hundred comments that morning, an
all-time record.

This is amazing. We are history, people. Congratulations!

Who wants to predict when we will breach $10,000? My bet is June 2018, once we pass bitcoin.

This is only the beginning, everyone is just getting here. Hold onto your butts.

I forced myself to log into my Gemini account. I sat perfectly still, a storm of possibilities swarming in my head. The anxiety reminded me of what it felt like going to Pill Hill.

I looked up at the clock on the mantle. Propped up next to it was one of our family Christmas cards. It'd been returned because of a bad address. I saw Eileen's handwriting, her smiley faces and the picture of my kids jumping on our bed, the annual back-of-card shot. Danny was so big now that he almost got a concussion on the ceiling when he executed his usual bed-jumping pose. I'm not particularly sentimental, but the whole thing, the whole family thing, was pretty much the best thing that had ever happened to me. No matter what passion I was following or demon I was attempting to overcome, Eileen had always kept the family running and the kids happy. I'd also take my share of credit. Together we were doing a great job, but especially Eileen. Maybe that was why she wouldn't allow herself to go down the same rabbit hole I'd been living in since I discovered crypto.

If ETH tanked, I'd have to tell Eileen and the kids that Dear Old Dad had fucked it up. I hadn't been able to secure their financial future, darn it. We'd had a lottery ticket, and I had squandered it. I'd tell them this would make a great story one day and then force out a laugh while I prepared for work at a job that would likely make me miserable. Eileen would have to go back to hustling for clients, which would be easier to do if she didn't know for eternity that it didn't have to be that way, that we almost had it all. But it had turned out to be a fever dream. Another one of my fucking fever dreams.

But I can't pretend that I'm a perfect television family man, immune from selfish passions. Of course there was another part of me that didn't want to be wrong. Maybe this was even more important. I couldn't imagine being a loser again. But still, Flip Side said there was more glory in our future.

On January 2, ETH hit $900. It had doubled in value over the past thirty days. It was up 10,000 percent in one year. It was among the fastest rising billion-dollar-plus assets in history. That day, thousands of new people joined r/EthTrader. But I was there first.

Watching the greedy masses pile into ETH reminded me of the famous battle scene from *Braveheart*. The hordes rush forward, lances ready. They are screaming, and their horses are at full sprint, snot shooting from their snouts. The defenders sit ready, not moving, calm, almost. They can't raise their pikes and shoot their arrows until they see the whites of the barbarians' eyes. They await the signal and want to die, because they might die, and why the hell haven't they shot yet? Still, the attack moves ahead at full clip, deranged faces twisted with mania and fury, insanity bleeding from every murderous movement. THEY ARE RIGHT ON TOP OF US.

Now.

With the dog now asleep next to me, recovering from my verbal lashing, in the middle of the day, as hunched retirees walked by the front window and *Butch Cassidy and the Sundance Kid* played muted on AMC, I sold 11,000 ETH, 72 percent of our remaining stack, at an average price of $915, netting $10 million. After paying taxes, with the amount we already had in our bank, we had enough.

I couldn't wait any longer. I'd done it cold-blooded, my rational brain in charge, no soundtrack playing in my soul, Flip Side screaming obscenities as I stuffed him back into the closet. I still had about 4,000 ETH, which we would hold for the long term. But I was no longer a whale, a beautiful maniac.

Eileen was still in Boston with the kids. I sent her a text: *We are done.*

CHAPTER TWENTY-SEVEN

WATER COLORS

In those days after the sale, before Eileen and the kids returned, I thought about my place in the family. I now entertained the idea that I was the most prominent person in my bloodline. It wasn't so much that I'd made the money. It was how I'd done it. I couldn't get over it. I recognized this thought as the first sign that I could become a serious douchebag. Maybe I already was one. It also made me think that I could blow it all if I wasn't careful.

I thought again about my grandfather, the man who'd died of a stroke at work. I'd always related to him, though he'd died twenty years before I was born.

Leaving everything behind and going to a new country was a drastic move. Like mine, his big gamble paid off. He hit the jackpot. He achieved the American Dream, not a Kennedy-sized dream, but a pretty damn good one.

My grandfather's drinking had been a shadow over him all his life. He was able to abstain for long periods, but when he had the first drink, he might go on a bender and disappear for days.

In America, he was sober for years. Then, at my aunt's wedding, he decided to have a glass of champagne. That was it. His Flip Side returned.

After he died, his obituary ran on the front page of the *San Francisco Express*. I don't know much more about him because my dad couldn't talk about his father without tearing up, taking a slug from his vodka soda, and changing the subject. It seemed to me that the two of them had unfinished business.

I wonder if my grandfather had declared victory before taking that fateful celebratory drink. Unquestionably, his dreams had come true. He had a postcard life in America. He may have thought his demons were vanquished for good. The illusion must have been strong.

I'd have to be careful if I was going to survive.

CHAPTER TWENTY-EIGHT

THIS IS SPINAL TAP

Finally, after it was all over, Eileen caught ETH fever. The night she returned from Boston, we stayed up until two a.m. discussing the possibilities. We agreed to book a family trip to Africa. We considered the merits of buying a home in Santa Cruz. We discussed whether we should pay off the remaining $950,000 on our mortgage now or later. Life was suddenly off the hook. Every time we were on the verge of going over the edge and losing ourselves in this new wealth euphoria, the dog scratched at the door, demanding to be let in or out because we were making her nervous. Then we had to go to bed.

A tribe of advisors was waiting to help us navigate the waters of new money. I received a text from Carl, an acquaintance who works for a big financial advisory firm. He'd heard from my sister Kathleen, who was an old friend of his, that I'd made a killing. He asked me out to lunch. As our salmon and brussels sprout salads were being prepared, I told him what happened, spilling my guts about the actual dollar amounts for the first time to anyone. Since he was in finance, I figured the rules of polite conversation pertaining to money didn't apply, in the same way it's ok to tell your plastic surgeon you want a smaller nose or bigger boobs.

He hadn't always been so interested in talking shop with me. The prior year, I'd spoken with him at a family party. Since I knew he was in finance, I had asked him at the time if he was interested in crypto before giving him an earful. Now, over lunch, he admitted that back then, he'd wanted to pivot the conversation back to the weather. Of course he wishes he'd listened to me, he said.

Like the very best lobbyists I knew from my public relations days, Carl is a genuinely likeable guy.

His charm and skills allowed him to rise to the top, where his attention is reserved for people like the current version of me and Eileen. He offered to help us figure it out. Sadly, he didn't offer to pick up the tab for lunch. If that was "keeping it real," I was disappointed. I wanted to partake in a Conway family passion: free food.

It was time to pay off our house, so I walked the few blocks to Wells Fargo, where we'd always done our retail banking. This was where we'd gone to complain like peasants petitioning Caesar when they pulled our equity line ten years before. The teller's jaw dropped when she opened our personal checking account and saw the twelve million-dollar balance. She asked if I had a private banker.

"Isn't that you?" I asked.

"No!" she said, as if I was being preposterous.

She disappeared and then ushered in the private banking manager, Gene, a petite, impeccably dressed, and overly polite man who took my hand and said we'd be working with him from now on. He was focused exclusively on servicing high net worth individuals. Unbeknownst to me, there was a separate space within the bank where I could now do my banking away from normal people.

He gave me his support line which I could call at any time, night or day, if I was experiencing a problem or presumably if I just wanted to talk. I had a vision of calling him late at night and asking, "Hey, what do you think of all this fucking money we have?"

We were now high-net-worth individuals and would be treated with proper respect and deference. He reversed the wire charges for some personal business we'd done a month before. I was thrilled and thanked him.

"No, it is the least we can do," he said.

There was only one uncomfortable moment, which happened when I was sitting in the private banking lounge chatting with Gene while he finished updating our account. He said he had two simple questions. First, had this money come from drugs or any other illicit activity? And second, was I involved in money laundering?

These rude questions coming when they did, as our conversation seemed headed toward Gene offering me a master-of-the-universe certificate, were jarring and unpleasant. I think Wells Fargo was employing the same strategy they use at my mother's retirement community to weed out those with dementia. Residents are required to take an annual mental acuity test to determine if they are losing their marbles. The test is forty-five minutes long and spans four different competency areas. When the ordeal finally appears to be over and the resident exhales, the administrator says something like, "Great job! Now relax. I just have one more question. Can you help me out? Good! Here it goes. If you have a newspaper, what on earth would you do with it? Put it in the washing machine? Eat it for a snack? Or read it?" It's one final question to see if they've gamed the system somehow. Wells Fargo wanted to know if I was a bandit. Of course, I told them I'd eat the newspaper as a snack, with a nice Chianti.

Even Gemini was wondering how the hell I got all of this money. I received this email from them out of the blue:

Hello Daniel Conway,

A review of your recent account activity showed high transfer values, including large ETH deposits. I see that you've indicated in your account profile that you are in Public Relations. Please provide the following information:

1) Please provide a recent pay-stub, the name, and a link to your employer.

2) What is your source of funds used to purchase cryptocurrency?

3) What is your history in trading cryptocurrency?

4) If you are an early investor in crypto currency then please provide documentation which supports your early investments.

5) Please provide any additional information regarding the source of funds or any other examples you can provide to support your account activity.

Please respond as soon as possible to avoid your account from becoming frozen

Regards,

Team Gemini

Since there are few mandated regulations for crypto exchanges like there are for traditional banks, Gemini was using its own algorithms to detect weird activity. The questions cast a broad net and amounted to *What's your deal?* I told them my history, showed proof, and was set free. In the back of my mind, I wondered if the email itself was a scam. That's life in crypto—you never know if you are emailing with a Gemini service rep or a dog smoking a cigar, headed to Malta with your sweet ETH.

Speaking of Malta, I talked to two slimy characters who run a tax haven in that country. I got their contact information from a friend after I complained about my 37 percent capital gains bill. He said that a partner in his firm avoided all sorts of taxes by offshoring his money. I am a community-focused liberal who believes everyone should pay their fair share, but I was willing to make an exception in this case. When I told the Malta guys I'd made my money from crypto, they took that as a soft yes that I'd go with their sketchy program, considering the obviously shady nature of my funds. They claimed their solution would save me millions in taxes. If the laws stayed the same. If I agreed to lock up my money until I was fifty-five. If I was still living. If these nuts hadn't run away with my money by then. No, thanks.

We stuck with the guy who brought us to the dance for our money management. Sean and the staff at Ensemble switched into a new gear. Their clientele was comprised of individuals with more than one million in liquid wealth. Most had much more than that. They were well prepared to educate us on the new normal and what we needed to be thinking about.

I figured we'd want to fully fund our kids' 529 college accounts and pump money into our IRAs. But that is actually what people do when they are trying to *accumulate* money. We now had a new priority: wealth maintenance and transference to the next generation. If we succeeded, our children would become the dreaded trust funders. An image flashed through my head. Jagged lines of cocaine on our dining room table. Jay crumpled under the table, blacked-out drunk. Annie posing nude by the pool as her latest boyfriend took pictures. Danny shooting his solid gold gun out back. Me prostrate like Joe Kennedy upstairs, in the final stages of ALS, a stream of dribble running down my chin. Eileen at Disneyland Paris with her new husband.

At least none of them would end up as Dilbert. We were actually pretty confident they would be ok. They each have their own little achievement hang-ups and neuroses, which might drive them forward even if they have big bank accounts someday. Plus, Annie would never pose nude by the pool. We don't have one.

It is beyond dispute that we now have a lot of money. But the pull of getting more cash, becoming richer, can't be underestimated. We still have 4,200 ETH. If it goes to zero, our U.S. dollar-delineated nest egg should be enough on its own for us to be set for life without having to work again. But if we had twenty million, we wouldn't even have to do the math. There would be no question.

I still want more money, because that primitive part of me still isn't sure we'll be ok, despite rational thinking. Plus, there is a certain sheen to twenty million dollars. It's beyond wealthy. Even though it's a merit badge neither Eileen nor I necessarily are striving for, it has a powerful, seductive attraction. Even a teetotaler will get hooked on heroin if you shoot him up every morning. So we need to hold on tight, because we are now traveling with the Ring, and it could quickly turn into our precious, ingratiating itself like a new dog or religion.

We allowed ourselves one big indulgence, right off the bat.

Eileen and I visited the Audi dealership to look at Q7s, the sport utility vehicle with a third row. Honestly, it was about time. My Volvo, which I had written a blog post about, three years prior, had only deteriorated since. It had broken knobs, no air conditioning, a backseat door that no longer opened, and a radiator that leaked and needed to be filled manually once a week. I felt like a working-class hero every time I topped it off.

At first we considered getting another Honda or Toyota, but ultimately, Eileen wanted the Audi. I liked the idea of her joining the naughty bitches jamming around town in their yoga pants and fancy cars.

The Audi salesman asked if we'd be leasing or financing the car, giving me the perfect opportunity to tell him we'd be paying in cash. Then, during small talk while we were filling out forms, he mentioned that he'd been breached in the recent Equifax hack. That allowed me to say, "Don't worry, blockchain is going to solve all of that."

He looked up from his papers, grabbed his phone and said, "Well, I have my crypto right here."

That was a damn near perfect assist, a textbook bridge, allowing me to say, "That crypto is how we're buying this car."

And then, to Eileen's dismay, we talked crypto. He owned ETH, Litecoin and TRON. I knew that TRON was widely considered a scam. I told him he should look into it.

He said, "Yeah, I just bought some because it was only a few cents."

He's like a lot of noobs who flooded into crypto in 2017, people who don't understand market cap in relation to the number of coins in circulation, and instead simply hope there is some chance a random coin can rise to twenty thousand dollars, "just like Bitcoin."

There didn't seem to be enough hours in the day to process what had happened to us.

During these initial days, when I hadn't yet told a lot of people about what had happened, I looked for opportunities to share my good news with strangers. The lady at Home Depot asked if I was off work. "No, I don't work. I'm writing a book about my experiences in crypto."

The dentist apologized for starting our appointment a little late, allowing me to say, "No worries. I'm writing full-time these days, so I have a flexible schedule." I was practically begging for a follow-up question. I wanted to tell humanity that I was loaded while pretending like I didn't care.

My friends had no inkling of how much money we'd made. They knew I was up a lot, but no one dreamed that I'd literally bet the house on crypto. If I had told them I'd made $200,000, that would've been a big deal. Sharing the good news has been difficult. In theory, the discreet and proper thing to do is keep quiet and not say much. But how am I supposed to answer when a good friend asks, "How are you doing?" or "What have you been up to?" or "Where are you working now?" I find it hard to tell only part of the story or be vague about what's happened. Imagine discovering a family of big-foots dressed in tuxedos while camping, and when you are asked about the trip, only being able to say that you whittled a stick.

My friends are equal parts happy for me and devastated. We'd always compare notes about work and our dream of getting out of the rat race. Everyone, including Eileen, thought my constant talk of finding an escape was the rambling of a loveable loser, an aspect of my awkward charm. Perhaps on my deathbed, I'd make a crack about finally finding a way to leave my job. Now that I'd actually escaped, I missed those discussions. I felt like a traitor. I'd obviously not trade what happened for anything, but at certain times, it was a little sad.

I also thought about Maureen. She had always struggled with money, and I could have helped her if I'd had this money back then. But more importantly, she would have loved the ride. My mom, Kathleen, and Joey had all jumped on the ETH train and made a load of money. One night we all went out to dinner wearing matching Ethereum t-shirts. Getting rich with those you love was an insanely great and totally improbable family chapter. But Maureen was already gone.

***

After buying the Audi, we had to drop some fabric off at Annie's friend's house in San Mateo. She knew Rebecca from sewing class. So we all piled in for a drive in the new car, which we'd literally just brought home. We told Annie not to say anything when she went in. Of course, it was the first thing she said. The whole family came outside. I'd parked one house down to ensure they couldn't see the new car through the window. I didn't want them to think we drove over to show it off. They said they liked it. Rebecca's dad, Stan, told me I looked ten years younger. God, this was excruciating.

It dawned on me that, up to this point, the people we were most comfortable with occupied the lower rungs of the upper middle-class lifestyle in our area. The Taylors, Fosters, and Sullivans were by and large like we used to be: just barely financially stable. With our windfall, we'd been transformed. On paper we were now more like the Pattners, Vices, and the Shiners—the upper crust of our area, with trust funds or big tech money and the cars to prove it. We used to be close to some of these people years earlier. But as they graduated to fancier bottles of wine, more expensive jeans, and vacations to all of the right places, we'd drifted away. To be honest, we resented them. We didn't feel as comfortable in their company, and the fault was mostly ours.

As I talked to Rebecca's dad, I remembered how we compared notes over the years about the pressures of living in this area. I could feel the distance between us. I'd lost my bearings. I realized I was going to have to dance around my new reality. Even if he couldn't care less—and he probably didn't—I did. I couldn't bear to talk about the decision we'd been weighing about whether we'd tour Eastern or Western Europe that summer. One of the bittersweet feelings about making a bunch of money is that you can't bring your friends with you.

***

I don't pay attention to small expenses like I used to. Eileen had a handyman come over to do a few projects the other day. Normally, I'd give this guy a strong handshake to make sure he knew I was aware of what was happening. I might be too lazy to manage these projects and too feeble and stupid to do them myself, but I'd be there to monitor the estimate, you got that, Tex? Then I'd have a hissy fit when Eileen agreed to the work before asking how much it was going to cost. Now, I let it go.

Doing something so right that it changes your life is exhilarating, but it is also uncomfortable. The other night, I was making dinner for me and the boys. I cracked an egg on toast, the first step in making a Popeye sandwich. Danny asked whether I'd ever considered using egg whites. In response, I laid out my nutritional philosophy. I noticed I was cogent and persuasive. I could have been a TV dad from the 1950s, perfectly rational and self-confident, with a rapt, respectful audience.

Later that night, he said he wanted to sign up for Apple Pay. And there I was again. This time I sounded like I had a degree in economics with a minor in psychology. I explained how cryptocurrency will send Apple Pay to the trash heap where it belongs.

It feels uncomfortable, like I've left home and am pretending to be someone else. Sometimes it's too much, and I'm tempted to close the blinds, make a fried ham sandwich, and binge watch *The Godfather* trilogy.

I see why lottery winners blow it all. They are drawn back to the familiar. And the suddenness of our windfall felt like winning the lottery.

But the mania that led me to crypto was fueled by a big idea beyond riches. It was based on a belief that cryptocurrency based on decentralization was so disruptive that it could create a new free and open Internet, reshuffle the economy, and change the pecking order. In that light, decentralization is far more than a way to get rich—it is a vehicle to blow the whole thing up and let the outsiders like me succeed. The ones with the strange personalities, uneven skill sets, and unrecognized talents. The ones with sporadic confidence. The introverts. The ones who get passed over for promotion in centralized corporations where flaws and insecurities are identified and punished.

That's why I took the risk. Yes, it was about securing a future for my family, but like Walter White, this was about me. I wanted to win. I wanted to pass all of those corporate warriors who got promotions over me and also those people more emotionally healthy who seemed to be better at living a happy life. So I took the ultimate gutsy shortcut to the top, and now I can look down and see all of the corporate warriors, poseurs, and those just plain better than me, those smarter, better looking, better smelling, more grounded, more loving. They are climbing up. I'll tell them, "Good to see you, boys. I took the back way."

***

Considering my newfound self-prominence, I was anxious to get to YouTube headquarters in San Bruno for an important meeting a few weeks after our cash-out in January 2018. I tried to rest my mind, watching the sights go by as I drove. I needed the meditation to pull myself away from the Reddits and a Twitter feed filled with cryptocurrency mania. I needed an escape from my own mind, which had become addicted to speculation, panic, and euphoria. I was trying to even out and re-engage with the world as a normal person. I was ascending back to real life, like a diver slowly rising from a treasure ship deep on the ocean floor.

I constantly thought about what had happened, and I was getting sick of it. Eileen didn't seem to have the same problem. She hadn't been consumed with it like I had. It was easier for her to process and go about her business, albeit with more family trips, no money concerns, and the ability to write the novels she'd always dreamed of publishing. I feared that it had all happened too quickly for me, creating a permanent glitch in my brain. Like Holder from *Game of Thrones,* perhaps I'd only be able to say or think one thing for the rest of my days. In my case it would be, "ETH WENT TO THE

MOON, ETH WENT TO THE MOON, ETH WENT TO THE MOON."

My meeting would be a good distraction. As I pulled into the parking lot, I identified the van parked in front of YouTube where my fat test would be administered. I'd been experimenting with a ketogenic diet, although I hadn't been strict about it. If done right, this diet melts the fat away. I wanted to see how I was doing. After lying in my underwear for five minutes in the back of a covered flatbed, I sat down in a lawn chair and waited for the results. A muscular young guy approached with a clipboard and pulled up a lawn chair next to me. He showed me the results. He'd probably given this talk a thousand times. This was not uncommon, he said. It boiled down to, "Don't panic, but your internal organs are encased in fat."

When my sidewalk consult was done, I stood up and concluded, "Fuck it." Whatever I was doing wasn't working, so I might as well regroup with a feast at the sushi restaurant in the strip mall next door. Once there, I ordered a large Coke, a jumbo bento box, and a separate order of spicy tuna rolls. Let me be perfectly clear: money was no object, nor were dietary restrictions.

Three YouTube workers on their lunch break were sitting next to me, and I could hear their conversation. The outfit I had on was fancier than pajamas but more casual than shorts and a tank top. Considering the way I slurped my miso soup as if nobody was watching, I wasn't likely a professional. They spoke freely.

They were gossiping about work. One of them couldn't stand a new co-worker who was above him in the pecking order.

"You know me. I told him straight up. If you are going to work on the launch, you need to know what's GOING ON WITH THE LAUNCH," he said. "So he said he's going to call a meeting and asked if I would join. Let me see—how about, NO!"

The lady at the table was hedging her bets. She was friends with the complainer but also an apologist for the new guy. She ripped her wooden chopsticks apart and rubbed them together to scrape off any splinters. "He definitely has a ways to go," she said. "At least he's gotten better since last month. Did you know they put him in charge of the Vegas event?"

The third guy, who was about to put a piece of sushi in his wide open mouth, pulled it back and looked at her. "Really? I thought Sue was doing that."

"No," she explained. "It was given to the new guy, and no one knows why."

God, I was relieved to be away from this bullshit. I'd had a million conversations like this over the course of my twenty years in corporate America.

The problem isn't the people. The problem is the rules they are forced to play by. In a *Forbes* article, Vitalik said it best, as usual. "If crypto succeeds, it's not because it empowers better people. It's because it empowers better institutions."

While Ethereum has made me rich, will it ever provide a viable alternative to the despair that many of us feel in the modern workplace? Will it ever meaningfully disrupt the corporation, allowing people to avoid the organizational structures and corporate cultures that make many of us miserable?

Will public blockchains run by cryptocurrency hand the Internet back to the people? Facebook, Amazon, Apple, and Google—plus scores of others who created what is called

Web 2.0 continue to play loose with our data and have made the Internet one big gated community.

The other day, I was talking to my friend Steve outside our kids' third-grade classroom. We had been engaged in a month-long conversation about blockchain conducted in fifteen-minute snippets on the soccer sidelines, in line at the Harvest Festival, and at the dog park. He is a vice president at a prominent cloud-computing software company. He'd followed the mania about bitcoin and ETH, and he was interested but reserved judgement. As the bell rang and the air filled with the sounds of screaming children, he gave me the news.

"You'll be happy to know that we are looking at blockchain," he said. "We've started a taskforce, and I'll send you the note. I wouldn't get too excited yet, because I doubt it will go anywhere, but I thought you'd want to know."

The usual suspect tech companies have become so complacent in their identity as disruptors, so smug in their ability to determine what is innovative and edgy, that they don't realize that crypto is coming to disrupt them. If your company makes a lot of money running proprietary software from a server farm, ten thousand nerds are trying to figure out how to put that same software on a blockchain where people like you and me can become owners by buying the token. A million corporate task forces aren't going to stop that.

CHAPTER TWENTY-NINE

NEXT

I n mid-January 2018, ether and every other cryptocurrency crashed hard. The crash intensified as the year went on. ETH hit a low of $80 on December 1, 2018, an 88 percent decline from its price when I sold the bulk of our shares at $915 and a 95 percent decrease from its brief, all-time high of $1,400 on January 14, 2018. Bitcoin hit a low of $3,295, an 88 percent decrease from its all-time high of $20,000.

The bubble has popped. As of this writing, in January 2019, we are in a bear market, and no one knows how long it will last. The mania that led to the run-up in 2017 was too much, too soon, and crypto has given back the majority of its gains.

Crypto has been through two cycles like this before, in 2012 and 2014. It isn't pleasant, but I'm not at all pessimistic about the future. I follow hundreds of crypto developers on Twitter, and the activity level is as high as ever. An army of zealots is continuing to build the infrastructure, consumer-friendly interfaces, and scaling solutions that will fuel the next phase of growth.

The Brave web browser, which runs on the Ethereum blockchain, has more than one million downloads. Coinbase has added forty-nine new coins, expanded globally, quadrupled in size, and is valued at more than six billion dollars.

My former client, BitGo, had a great year despite the crypto winter. They introduced a professional-grade custody solution for institutional investors and extended their multisig wallet to support sixty-two crypto assets, many of them tokens on the Ethereum blockchain that power dApps. They also landed a forty-five million-dollar funding round. (I can only hope they found someone to write those data sheets.)

It is during these times of fear, uncertainty, and doubt that critics say blockchain is a solution looking for a problem, that it is a false panacea that seduced a herd of naive dreamers despite having no mainstream use beyond speculation. I'm certainly one of those dreamers.

My inspiration comes from one of the more difficult block-chain endgame promises: that it will disrupt the corporation. There are dozens, hundreds, maybe thousands of other use cases that have lit a fire under developers and dreamers all over the world. Some are inspired by how blockchain could enable fraud-proof philanthropy by validating the proper distribution of funds. Some believe crypto micropayments will save independent journalism. Some are driven by the promise that blockchains will protect elections and ensure every vote is legitimate. Some say blockchain will eventually disrupt government itself.

Skeptics complain about blockchain not yet having users or uses. But that's because the technology makes things that were previously impossible, possible. It requires imagination and faith to see the future.

It's no surprise that people have a hard time wrapping their minds around the concept of decentralization. Centralization is all we've known for a very long time. It's hard to imagine any other way. But that wasn't always the case. For the first hundred years of the United States of America, for example, the key debate among policy makers and citizens was whether the country should be centralized. Jeffersonian Democrats advocated for a national economy based on decentralized farmers and shopkeepers, versus the centralized control of strong national banks, what we call Wall Street today.

I'm not advocating for a Maoist reordering of the world. And I'm not a libertarian. I think governments play an important role in society. I'm bringing this up simply as a reminder that decentralization used to be a reasonable priority for the common man and woman. Since the centralization of the Industrial Revolution, up until the invention of Bitcoin in 2009, it is a concept that has almost completely disappeared from thoughtful debate outside of academia.

Public blockchains based on cryptocurrency have reintroduced decentralization as an organizing principle worth exploring. Could solutions to problems like global warming that require broad consensus across the globe, which no single government can solve on its own, be enabled through blockchain? Yes, they could.

Whether it takes years, decades, or a century for blockchain to enter its prime is not a question I'm prepared to answer. But I believe it is a good thing, an amazing thing, that Satoshi Nakamoto's invention offers us a new tool to address some of the most important problems facing the planet.

Who exactly will use blockchain, and in what way? The better question is: what is possible? If we don't thoughtfully ask, we could end up sounding like President Rutherford Hayes in 1876, at the dawn of the telephone age, an invention that extended the reach of the modern corporation. Of the telephone, he said, "An amazing invention, but who would ever want to use one?"

***

No one asks me about crypto anymore. This is not just a drop, a correction, it's full-scale capitulation. Friends ask me if I got out in time. Yes, I did, but it doesn't have the same luster as when I was rich and RIGHT. I'm back to running on normal gas rather than jet fuel.

Long-term, I know I will be right about crypto again, but that's not the point. I need to make the kids dinner, go see a movie, and replace the filters on the furnace. Drug-free, alcohol-free, and free of crypto mania or other manias. What do I need to prove, anyway? Our life is pleasant as hell. We take a lot of trips, eat good food, sign the kids up for any damn lessons or programs they are interested in. A very good life, by almost any measure.

I am thinking about these things while I stare across the River Suir from the porch of our house in County Waterford, Ireland, looking across to County Wexford, that place from my family's past that I still associate more with leprechauns and legends than real life, even though we now own a home here.

Eileen and I purchased this house from her cousin Colman Murphy. He was diagnosed with pancreatic cancer in late 2017 and wanted to sell the house to us before he died. Colman was a well-known architect who designed and built the famous St. Stephen's Green Mall in the heart of Dublin. He was Jay's godfather and one of Eileen's closest relatives. The opportunity to purchase this beautiful home and provide Colman the liquid cash he needed to deal with his illness presented itself at a time when we miraculously had the money to do it.

The house is big and beautiful, right out of *Architectural Digest*. It is sunny and modern, on a full acre of beachfront property. Massive ships silently pass by the river on their way to port in Waterford City. Eileen and I are getting our Irish passports. We are citizens of the world.

On this morning, I look back through the window and see Eileen and the kids sitting on the big couch in their pajamas, reading their books, well rested. My books are on the table, ready for me.

There is a book on jiu-jitsu. I imagine my path to black belt and anticipate that I'll eventually show up at our friend's house parties fully ripped, looking like a Greek god, with all of the wives staring at me while I make my way to the hors d'oeuvres table to get some vegetables and meats.

There is a book on open water swimming. I have visions of becoming a master swimmer, a freak of nature in middle age, taking long swims in the ocean and outlasting bigger, supposedly tougher men.

The books are resting on the *Irish Times*. That morning, I read about yet another shooting back in America. I imagine that if I were there, I'd jump out from behind a corner, take out the shooter, then give interviews.

On the side table, still untouched, is a book on meditation I've been hauling around for some time. It is going to try to teach me to focus on the present. It will probably tell me that I don't need glory, that living in the moment is enough.

Tucked into the book is a schedule of twelve-step meetings in Ireland that I've been telling myself to check out.

I look through my binoculars one more time before going in. A stiff wind ruffles my remaining hair. Far up, beyond the meanderings of the river, I think I can see New Ross Harbor, the last thing my grandfather would've seen before leaving on a train for a port that would take him to the New World. I know this is impossible—it is too far away to see. But with the money and the big win, I feel like I can do anything. I can rewrite histories, I can heal wounds, I can set the record straight.

It's a struggle not to look for the next big thing. I don't want to ruin it all, no matter how many scores I still need to settle.

Flip Side is still with me. And no matter how much I want to pretend I've overcome him, I have not. He saved me. Like a cold-blooded CIA operative who goes rogue and is locked up, I'll keep him under cover until I need him for my next secret mission—something so insane, so unconventional, that only his twisted temperament could get it done.

ACKNOWLEDGMENTS

'd like to thank my wife Eileen. I clearly married up. Please stay healthy. I can't imagine life without you. Thanks also to Eileen for her editing and good judgment as a storyteller. And sorry for the crappy parts of our life that this book documents. I hope, at my funeral, you can at least deliver the old Irish faint-praise platitude that always cracked my dad up: "He was a good provider."

Thank you also to my three kids, Danny, Annie, and Jay. Having your dad write a book with this title can't be easy. Yet it's probably better than my previous working title, *Douchebag*. Thanks for your love and support—I couldn't have written this without you.

While I'm at it, let me thank the rest of my family, in particular my mom, Peggy Conway; sister Kathleen Kelly; and brother, Joey Conway. I'm very fond of you all. Thanks also to three important family members who aren't with us anymore: my dad, Joseph Conway; my sister Maureen O'Rourke; and my dear aunt and godmother, Nancy Hole, who passed away while I was completing this book. What I wouldn't give for another day with each of you. To all my family, you shaped who I am. After reading this book, you might have some explaining to do.

I had outstanding early readers who helped make this manuscript stronger in every way. Thank you to Clay Tingley, Rob Glickman, Cathy and Sean Stannard-Stockton, Mike Blickenstaff, Joe Schultz, April Rassa, and finally, my cousins and big supporters, Fred and Cathy Hutton.

Mary Kole was my developmental editor. I'd highly recommend her to any writer who can handle a thorough, brilliant and, if necessary, tough edit. Thank you also to copy editor Amy Wilson who helped me with the finishing touches.

My whip-smart blockchain researcher, Jack Cullen, found everything I needed, twice as fast as I thought possible. Evidence that I'm slipping, despite my vital and attractive appearance. Jack, you are going places. Thank you, my friend.

The team at the UPS store on Howard Avenue in Burlingame is outstanding. They helped with the numerous administrative projects involved in printing and shipping drafts to various readers and a million other things.

I wrote most of this book at two of my favorite places, Philz Coffee in downtown San Mateo and the Burlingame Public Library. When Philz was too quiet, I couldn't write. When the library was too loud, I couldn't write. Somehow, I finished anyway. Thank you for putting up with me for so long.

Thanks also to Katherine Boyle and Hilary Hinzmann for their contributions to previous versions of this project.

Thank you to Mr. Burg, my eighth grade English teacher who pulled me aside to tell me I could write. This was not long after the popular "Hate Dan Day" festivities. His kindness was a bright spot in my otherwise miserable life at the time. He was dying of a brain tumor but still took the time to work with me. I'll never forget it.

Finally, I'd like to thank the filthy animals of r/EthTrader. Crypto wouldn't be the same without you.

Reader: My website is www.danconwaywriter.com. There you will find my writings on crypto, life since our windfall, and other projects I'm working on. Thank you for taking the time to read this book.

CPSIA information can be obtained
at www.ICGtesting.com
Printed in the USA
FFHW011021190719
53709237-59399FF